INSIGHT MEDIATION LEARNING GUIDE

Cheryl A. Picard, PhD

LIBRARY AND ARCHIVES CANADA CATALOGUING IN PUBLICATION

Title: Insight mediation learning guide / Cheryl A. Picard.
Names: Picard, Cheryl A., author
Identifiers: Canadiana 20250318458 | ISBN 9781988657448 (softcover)
Subjects: LCSH: Lonergan, Bernard J. F. Insight. | LCSH: Conflict management. |
LCSH: Mediation. | LCSH: Insight.
Classification: LCC HM1126 .P49 2026 | DDC 303.6/9—dc23

Published by
LOOSE CANNON PRESS

info@loosecannonpress.com
www.loosecannonpress.com

DEDICATED TO

Dr Kenneth Melchin, Emeritus Professor, Faculty of Theology and Senior Research Associate, Lonergan Centre, Saint Paul University, Ottawa. It was Ken who first saw the potential of using Lonergan's theory of Insight to examine conflict and mediation through the lens of learning. And it was through his support that Insight Mediation developed into the theoretically informed practice it is today. I am most grateful for your friendship and mentoring.

ACKNOWLEDGEMENTS

Every good book is borne through the minds of many—the publication of this '*Insight Mediation Learning Guide*' was no different. In bringing this *Guide* to life, I had the privilege of drawing on the emergent and creative thinking and generosity of three extraordinary women, who gave freely of their time to refine its drafts and to shape its visual expression through the illustrations, cover, and design. I cannot thank them enough for their contributions, enthusiasm and commitment to advancing the practice of Insight Mediation. Elizabeth Sterritt is a bilingual accredited Family Mediator, Intergenerational Mediator and certified train-the-trainer in Intergenerational Mediation, and lead trainer for the Ontario Association for Family Mediation (OAFM) Intergenerational Mediation program. Jennifer Suzor is a highly experienced accredited Family, Child Protection and Intergenerational Mediator who has spent four decades helping families in the family justice system, and 20 years mediating full-time. She trains mediators in the Insight approach at *INSIGHTful Mediation Training*. Laura Taylor holds a Master of Laws in ADR from Osgoode Law School and has helped people navigate conflict over the past 30 years as a lawyer, mediator and arbitrator, who now devotes her energy to supporting transformative approaches to conflict as a mediator, coach and trainer.

I am also grateful for the following individuals who took time to provide feedback on an early draft of this *Learning Guide*: Dr Kenneth Melchin, Dr Marnie Jull, Dr Mike Stebbins, Mary-Anne Popescu, Jessica Alen, Jacinta Gallant, Linda Gunning, Harold Rosen, Krista Konrad and Cynthia Nantais. I am indebted to Shauna Young, Accredited Intergenerational Mediator, who so willingly undertook the task of editing the final text. Finally, thank you Robert Barclay for agreeing to publish this book.

Writing a book is a demanding and often uncertain journey, filled with moments of doubt and the temptation to set it aside. Through it all, my husband walked beside me with patience and unwavering faith. I am grateful for your steadfast support and enduring confidence.

Insight's Favour

Conflict lives where meanings part,
Where threat takes root within the heart.

Insight pauses, looks anew –
Reveals what fear has hidden from view.

Through understanding, minds unbind,
Interpretation redefined.

From threat to learning, paths extend –
Where knowing grows, and wounds can mend.

L. Taylor 2025

CONTENTS

INSIGHT MEDIATION LEARNING GUIDE
An Introduction
Learning is a treasure that will follow its owner everywhere (Chinese Proverb)

Welcome to this *Insight Mediation Learning Guide* and thank you for choosing to turn your mind to discovering more about the practice of Insight Mediation. The idea behind producing a practice-based 'guide' was to focus primarily on explaining and illustrating the distinct concepts, strategies and skills used in Insight Mediation. Specifically, the *Guide* focuses on what Insight mediators '*do.*' I also wanted to be sure you could easily locate the deeper theoretical explanations as to '*why*' they act as they do. With this in mind, frequent references are made to *Practising Insight Mediation* (PIM), published by the University of Toronto Press in 2016, including the page numbers where deeper discussions can be found.

The target readership and goal of this *Guide* is providing mediation trainers with an authoritative resource to use in their workshops to help them teach the practice of Insight Mediation. In addition, the *Guide* is written so as to be accessible to learners outside of guided workshops who may be interested in this mediation approach. Reading this *Guide* with a background in any model of mediation will no doubt invite you to open your mind to new ways of working with conflicting parties in mediation, perhaps even answering some of the elusive questions you ask yourself about how to be better at what you do.

The material found here is best suited for use in short two- to three-day practical training workshops, whereas *Practising Insight Mediation* was written as an academic text for use in college and university courses. Whether you are new to this approach, interested in learning more about what you already know, or yearning to brush up on your Insight skills to feel more confident using them, I am confident you will find this *Guide* helpful.

Experienced and successful mediators trained in other models with little or no background in the Insight approach, may well approach learning about Insight Mediation with some hesitancy. You might be wondering how much 'unlearning' you will be expected to do. You may worry that being 'clumsy' using unfamiliar skills will leave you looking less competent than you are in front of your peers. For these, and other reasons connected to identity and self-worth, becoming a learner of the Insight method may be challenging and even evoke feelings of threat. You are invited to notice these thoughts and emotions; they can provide deeper self-knowledge about how you learn. In addition, they will help you notice how parties learn, especially their blocks to learning manifested in their resistance to engage constructively in the mediation dialogue.

As a learner it will be beneficial to remain open minded and engage in asking curious questions. Not only will this benefit you, other learners stand to gain from your curiosity. Assume no questions are bad questions. Questions, along with doubts and challenges, expand knowledge for you and for others. Likewise, if you are in a workshop using this *Guide*, your questions will provide opportunities for the instructor to demonstrate Insight skills in 'the moment.'

Unlearning and relearning are as critical as continuous, acquisitive learning. Unlearning is about knowing what to give up. It requires self-analysis and having the confidence to discard what is no longer true, relevant, or helpful.

Throughout this *Guide* attention is focused on understanding yourself in relation to others. This is important as learning to learn about others requires we first learn about ourselves. The ability to understand our feelings and how we respond to others' feelings is a key element in Insight Mediation. This is because values evoke feelings and exploring these values and their requisite feelings teaches us about ourselves as individuals. In turn, self-knowledge helps us succeed as conflict professionals. As we become curious and critically reflexive of ourselves, we create space to become curious about those with whom we are in conflict, thereby enabling us to be more in touch with parties in a mediation.

Studies about self-reflection explain when we engage with our own thinking, we are able to think more critically, generate more accurate answers, and approach problems more creatively. Learning more about yourself to help you to learn more about others is the focus of Chapter Four. Being self-reflexive involves taking time to think about and evaluate your behaviours, thoughts, attitudes, values, biases, and conflict styles enabling you to be better equipped to help conflict participants be self-reflective.

You are best in charge of your own path to learning. This is why you are encouraged to keep a *Learning Journal* where you can record your thoughts, emotions, questions, and insights. Appendix A offers suggestions for using a *Learning Journal* to help you track the progress of your self-knowledge. Self-reflective practice in mediation is the process of being present with yourself and intentionally thinking about your actions, emotions, and motivations so you may learn from them. Michael Lang, a long-time and esteemed teacher of reflective practice, argues through reflective practice we increase our skills and knowledge and as a result we improve the quality of our professional practice. A *Learning Journal* is a tool for achieving this.

What You Will Find in this Learning Guide

Chapter One introduces you to the language of Insight Mediation. Chapter Two provides background to the development of Insight Mediation, along with a description of the theory of learning that guides an Insight mediator's practice. Chapter Three walks you through the method of Insight Mediation, while Chapter Four shifts the focus to a discussion of why self-knowledge is an important aspect of your work as mediators.

Each chapter includes a *Key Takeaway* that highlights significant ideas to help you reflect on and verify your understanding of that chapter. All four chapters include practice activities and reference to supplemental readings that can be found in Appendices C, D, E, F and G. The supplemental readings chosen are unpublished 'working papers' written by Insight researchers over the last few years. Keeping track of your answers to the activities and your reflections on the working papers in your *Learning Journal* is a great way to look back and applaud your advancement and success.

Insight Mediation is all about asking curious questions. With this in mind, the subsections in each chapter are formulated as a question in answer to the key question asked in that chapter. Below are some of these questions:

- *What are key Insight terms and what do they mean?*
- *When did Insight Mediation first emerge?*
- *What makes Insight Mediation unique?*
- *What is the learning theory behind Insight Mediation?*
- *What happens before and after mediation?*
- *What is the method of Insight Mediation?*
- *Why is understanding yourself important to your work as a mediator?*
- *What role does communication play in understanding more about yourself?*
- *How does knowing about conflict and personality styles help you notice your own responses to conflict?*

I hope you enjoy the experience of learning about yourself in relation to others as you engage in learning about the theory and practice of Insight Mediation; a method focused on helping parties move from an experience of threat that blocks [their] understanding to one of learning and genuine curiosity about others. I also hope your learning journey will generate enthusiasm for a deeper dive into the role of learning and curiosity - catalysts for becoming a skilled Insight mediator.

A Snapshot View of Insight Mediation

It is useful to point out that the material in this *Learning Guide* focuses on interpersonal and small group conflicts that involve disputes relating to family law, intergenerational and collaborative law, housing, policing, workplaces, communities, schools, churches, not-for-profit and volunteer groups, as this is where my expertise resides. I am confident that Insight theory has merit to a wider range of contexts, including large group and international conflicts. I look forward to hearing about future conflict professionals applying aspects of the Insight approach to these difficult situations. The statement below encapsulates how today's Insight mediators think of interpersonal conflict and their role in helping parties deal with it.

Interpersonal Conflict and the Role of an Insight Mediator

Interpersonal conflict emerges from the experience that one party's (the speaker) actions pose a *threat* to what *matters* to the other party (the listener). This *threat* experience triggers defensive conflict behaviour from the listener that *blocks* the listener from understanding what the speaker is saying. For the speaker, the listener's lack of understanding towards what matters to the speaker is a source of *threat* that feels like an attack to the speaker, and so they in turn also respond defensively. When these defend interactions are on-going, they block parties' curiosity and learning about each other.

Insight Mediation provides conflicting parties with a safe space to discover they may be, or are wrong about the other's intentions. When parties open up to letting go of previous understanding, or misunderstanding, they gain new understanding and real learning begins.

When the Insight mediator asks parties about an expected unwelcomed future and their cares that are being threatened, a new and less threatening understanding of the situation is discovered. This new understanding leads a party to speak in a manner not, or at least less, charged with judgement or attack-type behaviour, encouraging that party to explore the value they are protecting with the mediator.

A transformation in the conflict begins when the listener is able to open their mind to allow the operation of genuine questioning via authentic curiosity concerning the value the speaker is exploring. It is then the listener can safely discover there has been a misunderstanding, or they were wrong, about the speaker's intentions, and it is then when curiosity and understanding begin to emerge. Dialogue free of threat is when real learning ensues, and it is through learning parties discover they can choose to do things differently.

Reference Materials used in this *Insight Mediation Learning Guide*

Lang, Michael, *The Guide to Reflective Practice in Conflict Resolution*, 2019.

Melchin, Kenneth R., *Insight Studies: A Practice-Based Approach to Self-Knowledge and Critical Thinking*, Toronto: University of Toronto Press, 2025.

Melchin, Kenneth and Cheryl Picard, *Transforming Conflict through Insight*, Toronto: University of Toronto Press, 2008.

Picard, Cheryl, *Practising Insight Mediation*, Toronto: University of Toronto Press, 2016.

Picard, Cheryl, 'Learning about Learning: The Value of Insight,' *Conflict Resolution Quarterly,* 20 (4): 477-8, 2002.

Picard, Cheryl, 'The Origins, Principles and Practices of Insight Mediation,' *Revista de Mediación*, Vol. 10, No. 2, 2017.

Picard, Cheryl, and Janet Siltanen, 'Exploring the Significance of Emotion for Mediation Practice,' *Conflict Resolution Quarterly,* 31 (1): 31–55, 2013.

Picard, Cheryl and Marnie Jull, 'Learning through Deepening conversations: A key Insight Mediation strategy,' *Conflict Resolution Quarterly*, vol. 29, no. 2, 151-176, 2011.

Sargent, Neil, Cheryl Picard, and Marnie Jull, 'Rethinking Conflict: Perspectives from the Insight Approach,' *Negotiation Journal,* 27 (3): 343–66, 2011.

'Books are the training weights of the mind' (*Epictetus, Greek philosopher*)

Chapter One

THE LANGUAGE OF INSIGHT MEDIATION

All humans by nature desire to know (Aristotle, Metaphysics, 350 BC)

KEY TAKEAWAY

Everyday language is filled with similar words with different meanings. For this reason, Insight Mediation pioneers set out to define words with specific meanings to distinguish them from ordinary language. They believed doing this would avert conflation and confusion caused by using similar words with unalike meanings. This chapter contains explanations and examples of distinctive concepts, strategies and skills of Insight Mediation.

Whether this is your first time learning about Insight Mediation, or you have observed Insight mediators at work, you will have noticed they use distinct words to describe what they do. This is because pioneers of Insight Mediation believed creating clearly defined terminology of strategies and skills would help Insight practitioners minimize the conflation of Insight terms with similar everyday terms with different meanings. Building a vocabulary specific to the Insight method helps practitioners understand, and then use Insight principles, concepts, and skills correctly. This is what is meant by 'theoretically informed practice,' and what is behind the key adage: 'words matter.'

Beginning this *Guide* with an explanation and examples of prominent Insight skills, strategies, actions, or theoretical constructs is purposeful for two reasons.

First, as you read you will encounter these terms from the get-go. You will likely pause and wonder about their meaning, and I want to make it easy for you to learn what Insight mediators are referring to, and what they mean when they use a particular term.

Second, some *Insight* terms have differing meaning than the same words used in day-to- day language. As you begin learning about Insight Mediation, use this chapter as a resource to verify you understand the meanings of the terms we use in Insight Mediation.

Terms are listed here alphabetically and include corresponding page numbers from *Practising Insight Mediation* (PIM) where you will find additional information.

Finally, learners find it helpful to consider a specific conflict when constructing their own examples of strategies and skills or reviewing the examples provided in this *Guide*. Given learners of Insight Mediation work in a variety of fields of conflict (family law, child protection, intergenerational, community, workplace, collaborative law), I recommend drawing on an example of a conflict you mediated or were personally involved in to build your own case study from which to draw examples. Your 'conflict context' will allow you to engage with material relevant to your work and to your situation.

What are prominent key Insight terms and what do they mean?

BRIDGING (PIM 139)

Bridging is a connecting strategy that combines two communication skills: 1) listening to understand, which involves briefly restating the facts or reflecting feelings contained in what a party just said, followed immediately with 2) an open curious question intended to expand, deepen or develop on what is being said so to learn more about the experience, threat or care being shared.

Insight mediators use bridging to keep learning alive. When you reflect what you've heard before asking your next question, you signal that the party has been understood—reducing defensiveness and inviting continued sharing. A well-timed bridge can transform a tense exchange into a moment of meaningful insight.

Below are examples of effective bridging responses by the mediator: a reflection, followed by a curious question.

> *It is maddening when your co-parent is late dropping the children off despite your appeals to have them home on time; what is it that makes this so upsetting?*
>
> *The meeting was cancelled, and you are concerned about the delay, what problems do you anticipate the delay will cause?*
>
> *You were shocked to receive the letter from your manager about your performance, what made this so surprising and why were you so taken aback by it?*
>
> *You reacted with dismay when you heard what happened; what makes this news so disturbing?*
>
> *It is clearly worrisome to you that you may not get the promotion; what do you imagine will happen if you do not?*

BROADENING QUESTIONS (PIM 128)

Questions that *broaden* are open, genuinely curious, and focused on finding out more of the context surrounding the conflict, and parties' understanding of it. Insight mediators also use broadening questions when the conversation feels stuck or narrowly focused on a single issue. Expanding the frame helps parties recognize new connections that shift understanding. Using broadening questions to create and expand the context gives the mediator a fuller picture of what's been going on.

> *When did this happen?*
>
> *What did you do?*
>
> *How did she take it?*
>
> *Who else is involved?*
>
> *Tell me more.*
>
> *And, what then?*

BEING TRANSPARENT ABOUT INTENTIONS (PIM 134)

As a mediator, being clear and transparent about what you are doing and why demonstrates respect for the parties' self-determination—their right to make independent decisions without outside pressure. This approach supports parties in making informed, independent decisions and reinforces their role as primary decision-makers. Maintaining transparency is especially important when conversations deepen, as it helps prevent any perception that the mediator has a hidden agenda or is taking sides.

> *I am going to say something that might be surprising, make you pause a bit, or even leave you feeling a bit uncomfortable, but please know that my intent is only to open up some new areas of dialogue that might help the two of you move forward.*
>
> *My thinking is to slow down and take time to go over what you have been telling us about what really matters to you Sally. While this is happening, I will ask you Jacob to listen carefully, especially for new information that is different, and expands upon what you already know. After I verify that you understand correctly what Sally said, I will invite you, Jacob, to talk more about what it is that you care about.*

CARES (PIM 17-19)

Cares are deeply held beliefs that exist on personal, relational, and social levels. Cares motivate action, and are what motivate conflicting parties to become defensive, or defend, regardless if defending would be detrimental to their self-interest (PIM p. 17-18). The term 'cares' refers to more than the act of caring.

Personal cares involve our individual desires, goals, interests and needs.

Relational cares contain deeply held values about ours and others' identity, role, and beliefs, and about how we ought to act in relation to each other. They are revealed in our relationships and patterns of cooperation toward achieving goals that benefit all; they go beyond individual desires and needs.

Social level cares include normative expectations we use to judge what is right and just in society, for instance judgements about human rights and justice.

CURIOUS QUESTIONS (PIM 126-131)

Curious questions are open, sincere, non-judgemental and authentic explorations driven by curiosity that broaden and deepen on what is known to elicit new insights. They begin with *what, when, where, how, who* and to a much lesser extent, *why*, because a why question is often interpreted as an accusation or judgement that can produce defensive behaviour.

> *What is it that you are most concerned about?*
>
> *What is it about Lauren's coming home late that worries you?*
>
> *What more can you tell me about what happens when the schedule gets disrupted?*
>
> *How do you respond when you experience her behaviour as disrespectful?*
>
> *What is the most important request you have that you would like to talk about today?*

DECISION-MAKING (PIM 99-103)

Decision-making is the concluding stage of Insight Mediation. It is when mediation participants *use* the insights gained through understanding (having made sense of and verified what they learned) and then valuing (prioritizing what matters) so they can decide on the best actions to take as a way to resolve the cause of their conflict and improve each of their lives moving forward. The Insight mediator supports parties in reflecting on what has shifted for them during the mediation and encourages them to name new understandings before finalizing decisions. This reinforces ownership of the learning process and ensures any agreements come from genuine understanding rather than pressure to settle.

DEFEND RESPONSES (PIM 15-18)

Defend responses are used when individuals perceive unwelcome or dire outcomes. This type of response—a defend response—generates a sense of threat in others causing them to also defend. Defend responses include behaviours such as repeating one's point, becoming argumentative, making excuses, refusing to listen, shifting blame, becoming silent or withdrawn, being overly accusatory.

DE-LINKING (PIM 140-142)

De-linking occurs when, during conflict, it becomes clear that the information, assumptions, or interpretations parties have used to judge each other's behaviour are incomplete or inaccurate.

Through de-linking, mediators help participants distinguish present feelings from past experiences or imagined unwelcomed futures by expanding and clarifying what is currently known. When an incorrect or incomplete link is revealed, it often comes in the form of an insight or 'aha' moment. The curiosity generated from a de-link is used to form a more accurate understanding of the situation.

> *When you agreed to mediation you thought it would likely be a waste of time but clearly something has happened to change your mind. What did you hear that helped you change your mind, and where would you like to go from here?*
>
> *When we started this conversation, it was hard for you to listen, now you are fully engaged and asking genuinely curious questions, clearly something changed for you.*
>
> *You seem to have made a connection to something that happened before that is now less relevant and this is providing you some relief.*
>
> *You are really hurt by how the team interpreted your email because that was not the message you intended, what would you like to tell them now about what you were intending?*
>
> *You are recalling the time restructuring happened and jobs were cut, after listening to Simon's plans for streamlining the business, you seem less anxious, is this so?*

DEEPENING THE LEARNING CONVERSATION (PIM 43, 79, 132-134)

Deepening the Learning Conversation is a core Insight Mediation strategy that allows mediators to explore more fully the underlying cares or concerns that cause a party to feel threatened and respond defensively.

Deepening integrates several advanced communication skills, including *bridging* and *layered questioning*, to help make sense of what may initially seem confusing or contradictory. Through deepening, mediators guide the conversation toward clarity—helping speaker and listener understand what truly matters to each person and what is being protected, rather than allowing the dialogue to bounce reactively back and forth.

> *What is it about the way the two of you interact that you feel compelled to respond competitively yet you know it gets in the way of amicable conversation?*
>
> *You mentioned feeling dismissed—what more can you tell me about what that experience was like for you?*
>
> *What are his responses saying about his commitment to getting this settled, and what might be helpful now?*
>
> *When you doubt sincerity in your conversations with her what happens?*
>
> *What would you expect her to be doing differently if she really was sincere about no longer breaking curfew?*

Differentiating between Defend and Threat-to-Care Stories (PIM 28)

Differentiating between parties' 'defend' and 'threat-to-care' stories is essential as it helps the Insight mediator distinguish between lines of inquiry that produce new learning and new understanding from blaming and judgemental narratives that are likely to block the conversation. Threat-to-care or care stories contain information about what really matters to parties' (needs, values, identity). They hold information about what is being defended against. It is these stories that hold potential to bring about new understandings and new insights that pave the way for more fruitful conversations and less defensive ways of interacting. In conflict situations threat-to-care stories are rarely shared between the parties because they contain a sense of vulnerability.

In contrast, defend stories contain a party's justification for being right and entitled to have their way. They are closed stories with little room for change because there is a certainty of knowing all there is to know about the other's intentions so there is little reason to be open-minded or curious.

Distinguishing Between Hierarchical Levels of Values (PIM 45)

Distinguishing between parties' levels of value is key to how an Insight mediator observes, interprets, and responds in conflict. Individuals can hold strong feelings about one or more of these levels of value:

- Individual values – personal goals, desires, interests, and fundamental human needs.
- Relational values – normative expectations in relationships, institutions, or inter-personal cooperation that help meet collective needs.
- Societal values – beliefs and principles about life, society, or human nature that are subject to reflection and scrutiny.

Insight mediators often intervene in conflicts involving relational and interpersonal values within long-standing, deeply rooted relationships in families or groups. These relationships naturally carry normative expectations that can trigger strong emotional responses. Common values in these contexts include honesty, trust, respect, loyalty, open communication, shared goals, emotional intimacy, mutual support, parenting responsibilities, and broader principles about human interactions.

Insight mediators pay attention to which level of value a conflict is centered on. Recognizing whether a party is motivated by personal, relational, or societal values helps frame questions and interventions that are relevant, resonant, and more likely to generate insight rather than defensiveness.

DISRUPTING CERTAINTY (PIM 22, 27)

When parties are certain they already know everything about each other, curiosity is blocked, and opportunities for listening, learning and understanding are limited. True curiosity emerges when that certainty is disrupted, shifting attention toward exploring what is not yet known.

Insight mediators support this process by facilitating skillful communication: reviewing what is already known, highlighting new information, and ensuring it is accurately understood. They then help parties synthesize these new connections, opening the way for dialogue, listening, learning and understanding on new ground.

EXPLORING MEANING-MAKING, ASSUMPTIONS AND INTERPRETATION (PIM 136)

Conflict often arises from inaccurate interpretations, assumptions, or meaning-making. Expanding and correcting these understandings is essential to de-escalation and change.

Insight mediators pay attention to statements that imply certainty or judgement and explore underlying assumptions with open, curious questions to help parties uncover new insights and shift toward shared understanding.

In Insight Mediation, asking questions that explore assumptions, interpretations, and meaning-making is a core strategy. Examples of such questions follow.

> *How did you make sense of his reaction to your request?*
>
> *What are you hearing him say?*
>
> *What are you taking away from these discussions?*
>
> *What does it mean to you when the money does not arrive promptly?*
>
> *You made some assumptions based on what you were told, what were you expecting that did not happen?*

FEELINGS AS CARRIERS OF VALUES (PIM 44)

Feelings reveal what matters most to people, in other words, what they value. Insight mediators pay attention to feelings by noticing, acknowledging, and inviting parties to express their feelings then explain why they feel that way as a way to surface their cares.

Feelings in the present often connect to past experiences or fears about the future. Exploring parties' feelings help uncover what they care about and what they feel is at risk.

> *His comment that you have not been fully present at the meetings lately annoys you. Talk about this so we can understand your reaction.*
>
> *Has something happened before that leads you to make that conclusion today?*
>
> *Where does the fear that some of the Team may lose their job come from?*
>
> *You are clearly trying to stop something from happening. What is that something you think needs to be protected and why do you feel that way?*

FINISHING THE LEARNING CONVERSATION (PIM 137-138)

'Finishing' the learning conversation means staying with one party's threat-to-care narrative until it is fully explored—until there are no more questions to ask and the party feels heard and understood on that point. Unlike other mediation styles that focus on giving each side equal airtime, Insight mediators stay with one party long enough to uncover what truly matters before moving on. This happens once the conversation has shifted away from defensive reactions toward open dialogue. At this stage, new information is shared, misunderstandings are corrected, and parties begin to see each other's cares more clearly. If the listening party seems restless or uncomfortable, the mediator can reassure them they will have their turn to speak and be fully heard. Insight mediators stay with one speaker long enough to reach real understanding—they do not rush to 'balance' the airtime. Deep listening builds trust and opens the door to genuine learning.

> *You clearly want to jump in here, Tom, to correct what you hear Jack saying about your intentions and it can be hard to hold back. Remember I will give you the chance to speak without interruption once Jack has finished explaining his view. Please jot down important points to remember and we will get to you soon.*

HOPE QUESTION (PIM 29, 47-48, 73)

The 'hope question' is used at the start of mediation to help parties shift from defending their position to talking about what motivated them to come to mediation, and what they hope will be better in their life tomorrow if they are able to reach a satisfactory conclusion today. Creating a space where parties can explore their hopes is at the heart of Insight Mediation—it helps transform tension into possibility. Insight mediators ask the hope question early and with genuine curiosity. It sets a positive tone, signals safety, and helps parties move from protecting their positions to imagining shared possibilities. Further discussion about the 'hope question' can be found in Chapter Three, and a working paper on this topic is included in Appendix E.

> *So, what are you hoping will be better when you leave here today if you are able to have a conversation about the partnering arrangements that you came to talk about?*
>
> *You were motivated to come to mediation so something would change for the better in your life; what is it exactly you are hoping will be positively changed?*

INSIGHT (PIM 39-40)

An *insight* is an 'aha' moment when the light bulb goes on and we suddenly see something in a new way. It is a mental and physical experience—changing how we think *and* how we feel.

There are two types of insights:

- *Direct insights* connect and integrate what we are already exploring.
- *Reverse insights* challenge our current way of thinking and open a new path of inquiry.

Insight emerges through curiosity. Asking open, curious questions helps uncover new understanding about ourselves and others—and this process of learning is at the core of Insight Mediation. Insight mediators encourage curiosity by asking questions that expand or shift thinking. When parties experience the 'aha' moment, they often move naturally from defending to understanding.

LAYERED QUESTIONS (PIM 129 & 134)

Layered questions are a communication skill where each question builds from the answer to the one before it. They help the mediator go deeper into a party's interpretations, meaning-making, and the underlying threats and cares that shape their experience.

> Speaker asks: *You mentioned you wanted him to show evidence of his commitment to the welfare of the children; what would he have to do to show you this?*
>
> Listener answers: *He would have to be more respectful.*
>
> Speaker asks a layered question: *You are looking for him to be more respectful; what would being more respectful involve, and what would it tell you about his intentions?*
>
> Speaker asks: *You are uncertain about the new policy at work; what is it about the policy that troubles you?*
>
> Listener answers: *I am troubled by the lack of clear direction for how to deal with and who to talk to if the policy fails to resolve the issues the Team is currently experiencing.*
>
> Speaker asks a layered question: *You are looking for the policy to include what to do and who to go to if things do not improve; what is your worry if this is not included in the policy?*

LEARNING (PIM 35-42)

Learning in Insight Mediation is gaining new understanding that changes how we think and act. Listening, learning and understanding are at the heart of solving conflict. The Insight mediator's role is to create a safe space where parties can explore what matters to them and what feels threatened. When people realize they may have misunderstood the other's intentions, communication becomes unblocked, genuine learning begins—and change follows. Unlike approaches focused on negotiation or compromise, Insight Mediation emphasizes discovery. Learning here is not just about sharing information; it is a transformative process of insight that shifts feelings, perspectives, and relationships. Insight mediators foster learning by encouraging parties to explore what's new or surprising in what they hear—this is where change takes root.

LINKING (PIM 140-142)

Linking involves listening for and asking about how present behaviours and emotions are connected to past experiences and expectations of an unwelcomed or dire future. It produces direct insights into the cares parties are defending and reveals how their cares are linked to experiences of threat in the other party. Linking makes sense of how the values driving the conflict are influencing actions contributing to the situation.

> *It has been very hard for you these past few months not knowing what would happen if you let this situation with your co-worker go on any longer, and this is why you sought advice from your supervisor.*
>
> *You are clearly worried that your job is at stake, and that the difficulty you have been having with your co-worker Kim is escalating the problem.*

LISTENING TO UNDERSTAND (PIM 116-122)

The communication skill *listening to understand* has characteristics similar to active listening; however, it involves more than simply paraphrasing what you heard the speaker say or feel.

> *You have health issues that keep you from working and you are worried about how you are going to pay for your child's extra-curricular activities without being able to count on support from John.*
>
> *Your anxiety, along with your workload, has escalated due to Jolene being repeatedly late arriving for work, which is why you felt you had no recourse but to confront her about this.*

Listening to understand ensures the mediator is intentionally responsive to and acting in the service of the party speaking. Listening to understand also involves the mediator and the parties in the operations of learning as set out below:

1) *Experiencing & Noticing* involves noticing what we see, hear, feel, imagine, and remember, then questioning them.

2) *Understanding & Insight* draws on our cognitive map to make meaning of our senses.

3) *Verifying Understanding* involves wondering and questioning to discover 'do I have this right'; 'is there more to know?'.

4) *Verifying Valuing* involves reflecting on how much we know matters; how important is the information learned?

5) *Deciding & Acting* is about choosing if and how to respond to what we understand.

Listening to the Listener (PIM 20-22)

'Listening to the listener' is a core Insight communication skill that helps ensure one party truly understands what the other is saying. By asking the listener what they heard, the mediator can gauge whether curiosity and learning are taking place. In long-term relationships—such as families, workplaces, or communities—people often see themselves as the 'knower' and 'defender' of the truth. This can block curiosity and make it hard to hear or trust the others' perspectives. By checking in with the listener and asking questions about what they heard, the mediator helps uncover misunderstandings, challenge assumptions, and opens space for new insights and change. As long as the listener is certain of already knowing all there is to know about others' intentions, listening, learning and understanding remain blocked, and conflict behaviour is unlikely to change. Curiosity grows when certainty softens.

> *Your supervisor shared some of her concerns about your recent work, what are you hearing her say about these concerns?*
>
> *You have been listening for a while now about his view on what is urgently needed from the congregation, what are you taking away from what he is saying?*
>
> *She shared with us what is threatening for her at school, what is it that you are hearing her say about that?*
>
> *How are you understanding what he is saying about the lack of community housing?*

Noticing (PIM 24, 43)

Noticing is another core strategy in Insight Mediation. It means the mediator pays close attention to verbal and non-verbal exchanges—how parties speak, listen, and respond to each other. By observing these patterns, the mediator can tell whether parties are open to learning or still feeling defensive. Noticing requires being fully present in the moment and focused on what's happening *between* the parties. It also involves sharing your observations out loud and naming what you *see, hear,* and *interpret* from the interaction. This helps bring awareness to how the conversation is unfolding and invites reflection. When an Insight mediator notices tension, hesitation, or openness, they name it with curiosity. For example: *'I notice you paused there—what's happening for you in this moment?'* This helps deepen awareness and builds trust in the process.

> *I noticed you cringe when that last suggestion was made, what was that about?*
>
> *I hear the tone of your interactions getting louder, what is happening for you now?*
>
> *You both seem more relaxed and hopeful, is what I am noticing correct?*

OPERATIONS OF LEARNING (PIM 36-42)

The learning approach in Insight Mediation is grounded in Canadian philosopher Bernard Lonergan's work on insight. His operations of learning provide the theoretical frame and 'operating system' for what an Insight mediator does. Many of the Insight strategies and skills described in this *Learning Guide* are embedded in one of more of these five operations:

1) Experience and noticing.

2) Understanding and insight.

3) Verifying understanding.

4) Verifying valuing.

5) Deciding and acting.

PATTERNS OF INTERACTION

Patterns of interaction are the repeated ways people communicate—through words and body language. In Insight Mediation, this term refers to how parties consistently respond to each other during conflict. Insight mediators pay close attention to 'defend' patterns, such as refusing to listen, arguing, blaming, denying, or attacking. These behaviours aren't random—they are responses to feeling something important is being threatened. When Insight mediators notice a defend pattern, they do not view it as 'bad behaviour.' Instead, they get curious about what deeply held care or concern might be underneath it. That's where the learning begins.

RELATIONAL WORLD VIEW (PIM 48-52)

A *relational worldview* sees people as social beings who act and react in connection with others. Our behaviour is shaped by our environment—our culture, traditions, communities, and relationships—and, in turn, our actions influence those around us, often without us realizing it. Sometimes we even act based on how we think others expect us to behave.

Insight, Transformative, and Narrative approaches to mediation are all based on this relational view of human nature. In contrast, interest-based approaches see people as individuals motivated by self-interest. In Insight Mediation, we believe people are *responding more than intending.* This means their behaviour is a reaction to how they interpret a situation, not necessarily a deliberate plan to cause harm. By exploring those interpretations, mediators can help people understand what their actions are in response to. Being relational also means what we do today affects what happens tomorrow. How we handle conflict now shapes how we respond in the future—and what we learn today helps us grow.

When parties react strongly, Insight mediators remind themselves parties may be *responding* to what they perceive as a threat, not *intending* to harm. By approaching each reaction with curiosity instead of judgement—insight mediators open doors to new understanding.

RESPONSIVE INTENTIONALITY (PIM 31-33)

Responsive intentionality refers to the actions of an Insight mediator being intentional and based on their understanding of theories about human interaction and conflict. Their interventions are attentive to what parties say and do in the moment. Staying clear of leading parties toward a solution or guiding their stories, the mediator listens closely and engages with the parties in their time and with their 'story,'

Insight mediators do not follow a rigid formula or set of steps. Instead, they stay present and responsive to what is unfolding between the parties. Their questions are designed to help parties reconnect with their own curiosity and understanding—sparking insight, learning and understanding. Responsive intentionality is about meeting people where they are and helping them explore what matters to them. In no way being directive, an Insight mediator relies on social and psychological theories for their interventions, thus the term *responsive intentionality*. They are responsive to, and in service of the parties' lines of curiosity and understanding.

Insight mediators stay grounded in the moment through their 'self-talk', *'What am I responding to right now?'* This quick reflection helps ensure their next question serves the parties' learning—not their own agenda.

> *Why am I acting in the way I am at this moment in time?*
>
> *What did I notice that caused me to respond as I did?*
>
> *What theory of practice is guiding me now?*

SELECTIVE PARAPHRASING (PIM 29)

Selective paraphrasing means the Insight mediator is careful not to repeat or summarize a party's *defend story*—statements that blame, attack, or criticize. These kinds of stories often appear early in mediation when emotions are high. Instead, the mediator focuses on reflecting parts of the story that reveal the party's worries and what matters most to them.

This approach helps keep the conversation open and reduces defensiveness, allowing both parties to listen, learn and understand. When paraphrasing, Insight mediators self-talk asks, *'Am I repeating blame or revealing care?'* Focusing on what the speaker values rather than what they oppose shifts the tone from judgement to understanding.

> Instead of the mediator paraphrasing, *'As I hear it, the issue for you involves John's poor behaviour during the staff retreat last month'*, they might say, 'one *of the things we need to talk about is what happened at the retreat last month'*.
>
> Or, instead of paraphrasing what a party said this way, *'You felt betrayed by Simone when she went to the manager and complained you were purposely leaving her out of important Team meetings'*, the mediator might selectively paraphrase this way, *'who is selected to attend Team meetings needs to be discussed and clarified.'*

TRANSPARENCY (PIM 134-135)

Transparency is a strategy involving disclosing to parties the intentions behind the Insight mediator's actions. It is used to set parties at ease by letting them know there are no hidden agendas, secrets, or tricks being used, and that the mediator will be open and honest as they work to create learning and build understanding about parties' feelings and values.

> *This seems like a good to time to 'peel the onion a bit,' which means I will ask questions that will hopefully ensure we understand the full extent of your feelings and concerns. While I do this with you Sam, I will ask you Donna to listen intently for any new information that might change how you have been interpreting Sam's approach toward you. After this happens, I will do the same for you Donna and ask Sam to listen for anything new in what you are saying that might change how he has been viewing things leaving him wondering and curious. Do either of you have any questions or concerns before I proceed?*

THREATS-TO-CARES (PIM 17-19; 28; 43-44)

Threats-to-cares describe moments when what matters deeply to us feels at risk. When our cares are threatened, we naturally become defensive—our focus shifts from being curious or understanding others to protecting what we value most. Recognizing threats-to-cares helps explain why people behave the way they do in conflict. Understanding these threats is key to helping parties move from defending to listening, learning and understanding. When Insight mediators notice defensiveness, they look for the care underneath it and ask curious questions like, *'What feels at risk for you right now?'*

Using Insights Gained (PIM 138)

Using insights gained means the Insight mediator helps parties connect what they have learned about their threats and cares to their conflict behaviours—such as demands, closed-mindedness, or strong emotions. This skill allows the mediator to link or delink past experiences from present situations, helping parties make sense of actions or reactions that seemed confusing before. By using insights gained, the mediator ensures what has been learned through deepening conversations leads to more understanding and new ways for parties to interact.

When an insight emerges, Insight mediators name it clearly and connect it to what is happening now. For example: *'It sounds like feeling unheard in the past makes it harder to trust what's being said today.'*

> So, when Venessa came into your office waving your report in the air your first thought was, she was going to attack you in some way. This is why you went to talk to the conflict resolution officer even though the two of you have worked well together for a long time.
>
> Now that you have learned how late reports impact Vanessa's work, let's discuss what could work for both of you if this were to happen again.

Valuing (PIM 41-42)

Valuing is the stage of learning where we reflect on how much something truly matters—to ourselves and to others. It is about asking, *'So what?'* and understanding the importance we place on what we have learned. This stage often brings feelings to the surface, since emotions are closely tied to what we value. Learning is not a straight line—it loops back through experience, understanding and verifying, as we keep asking questions to help clarify what really matters.

When parties begin to show emotion or emphasize what is important to them, Insight mediators pause and explore it. They ask, *'What makes this part stand out for you?'* or *'Why is this important to you right now?'* These questions help deepen understanding of values and motivations.

Verifying (PIM 40-41; 139)

Sometimes, our insights can be wrong. That is why Insight mediators make sure the listener has truly understood what the speaker meant. Verifying is a core Insight skill grounded in curiosity and accuracy. It involves checking understanding by asking short, closed questions:

> *'Do I have that right?'*
>
> *'Is there more I should know?'*
>
> *'Have I missed something important?'*

These simple questions ensure learning is real and shared, not assumed.

> *Am I right in hearing you say what she is telling you now is news to you?*
>
> *It would be good for you to tell her what you hear her saying so that she can let you know if you have it right.*
>
> *Is that your full intention or is there more you want him to know?*
>
> *Are you finished speaking or is there more?*

Activities and Recommended Readings for Chapter One

Activity 1: *Who Am I in Conflict?*

In John Dewey's book, *How We Think (1933),* he says, *'we do not learn from experience…we learn from reflecting on experience.'* In this activity spend time reflecting on 'you' in conflict situations. Feel free to do this activity on your own or with others. The task is to gain self-knowledge by reflecting on the question *'Who am I in conflict?'* Below are some questions to help you get started. This activity is a great way to start writing in your Learning Journal (see Appendix A).

1. *What three things do I believe about conflict?*
2. *What metaphors, images, or expressions do I use to describe conflict?*
3. *What is my pattern of behaviour when involved in a conflict situation?*
4. *What do I like about my pattern; what works or seems effective?*
5. *What do I dislike about my pattern; what behaviours get in the way of being effective?*
6. *What worries or threatens me most when I am involved in conflict?*
7. *What would I most like to change about how I deal with conflict?*
8. *What do I want to learn; what knowledge and skills do I want to acquire, and what strengths do I bring to help me accomplish my learning goals?*
9. *What beliefs, behaviours, attitudes, and biases will I need to put aside to achieve my learning goals?*

Recommended Readings

Read the working paper: *An Essay on Learning, Unlearning and Re-Learning* written by Cheryl Picard and found in Appendix C (you will also be asked to read it again in Chapter Four). While reading this paper record your reflections, questions, or insights in your *Learning Journal*. To get you started, here are some questions to consider:

1. *What has been my experience in learning situations in the past?*
2. *Am I energized by learning or do learning situations stress me in some way?*
3. *How would I describe myself as a learner?*
4. *How do I react to new viewpoints that contradict what I already know?*
5. *Am I someone who easily lets go of what I know to try something new?*
6. *Do I welcome change or do I resist it? How do I know?*

Chapter Two

TURNING OUR MINDS TO LEARNING ABOUT INSIGHT MEDIATION

Learning to learn is life's most important skill (Tony Buzan)

KEY TAKEAWAY

Insight Mediation is grounded in Insight learning theory; a theory that Insight mediators use to provide a safe space for conflicting parties to discover they may have been wrong about each other's intentions. They do this by exploring each party's operations of experiencing, understanding, verifying, valuing and deciding with a goal of helping parties listen, learn and understand. Learning begins when parties open to releasing previous understanding to gain new understanding. It is through learning parties discover less threatening and less conflictual ways to interact with each other.

When did Insight Mediation First Emerge?

Insight Mediation emerged in the early 2000s from the joint work of Drs Kenneth Melchin and Cheryl Picard. We were interested in knowing more about what mediators are doing when they mediate. Of particular interest to us was the transformation that occurs when parties move from being stuck in conflict to collaborating to resolve it. To help answer this question we engaged with the ideas about learning and insight of Bernard Lonergan, a Canadian Jesuit priest. The results of our work, along with early foundations of Insight theory and its importance to conflict resolution and mediation work, are published in *Transforming Conflict through Insight* (2008). Most notable, is our exploration of understanding conflict work as learning; learning involving insights that produce discovery and shifts in feelings, perspectives and relationships.

After this work, I turned my attention on how Insight theory could clarify and expand the micro skills of Insight Mediation. *Practising Insight Mediation* (PIM) (2016) is the result of this work. PIM is a practice-based companion to *Transforming Conflict through Insight;* both available through the University of Toronto Press, Indigo and Amazon. In PIM, I describe *how* Insight mediators do their work, and *why* they do it that way. PIM also contains:

- In-depth descriptions of insight communication skills and strategies with links to social theories.
- A transcribed mediation simulation with an analysis of the mediators' interactions.

- A compilation of sample mediation documents.
- A self-assessment tool specifically designed for Insight mediators.
- Early research into the application of the Insight approach to other conflict contexts.

These two books unleashed a revolution in how Insight practitioners, especially mediators, regard, and respond to, conflict today. As interest in becoming a competent Insight mediator grew globally, Dr Picard and other Insight trainers focused on producing materials and workshops to meet the demand. This *Insight Mediation Learning Guide* is a part of this work. More specifically, it is a resource for mediation trainers teaching about the Insight approach to their learners.

What Makes Insight Mediation Distinct?

'Thinking about conflict intervention as a learning endeavour is not to suggest that, in Insight Mediation, solving problems or reaching agreement is unimportant – of course, they matter – but the way to solve problems and settle issues in dispute is through the process of learning something new.'

As you read this *Guide* you will learn one distinct characteristic of Insight Mediation is it draws on learning theory to explain conflict results from apprehensions of threat that produce defend responses which block understanding and learning. This differs from other conflict theories that attribute conflict to unmet needs, power struggles, resource competition, or opposing positions (PIM 14–15). Instead of relying on negotiation, conciliation, concession or compromise strategies to resolve conflict, Insight mediators focus their interventions on expanding what parties know about themselves in relation to others. At its core, the process helps parties uncover what is blocking them from expanding their understanding. When threats are removed, they can explore constructive and lasting ways to address their differences.

As a mediation practitioner, how you understand conflict impacts how you interact with parties in mediation. The Insight mediator's approach is based on understanding that:

Interpersonal conflict emerges from the experience that one party's (the speaker) actions pose a threat to what matters to the other party (the listener). This threat experience triggers defensive conflict behaviour from the listener that blocks understanding about what the speaker is saying. For the speaker, the listener's lack of understanding towards what matters to them is a source of threat that feels like an attack and so they, too, respond defensively. When these defend interactions are on-going, they block the parties' curiosity and learning about each other. Insight Mediation provides conflicting parties with a safe space to discover they may have been or are wrong about the other's intentions. When parties become open to letting go of previous understanding to gain new understanding, real learning begins. It is through learning parties discover they can choose to do things differently.

The following illustration depicts how conflict emerges:

Threat-based actions, words, non-verbal

Building on this understanding, changing a conflict situation requires parties to identify and understand how their threat experiences, defend behaviours and patterns of interaction are blocking their ability to listen, learn and understand what really matters to each other. The Insight skills of curious questioning, listening to the listener, and deepening defined in Chapter One are used by an Insight mediator to unblock communication caused by experiences of threat. When authentic communication is restored, parties are able to correct misinformation and absorb new information. The result is they become aware of each other, what the other cares about, and how this valuing is linked to their behaviour. The approach is different from negotiation approaches that seek resolution through compromise and collaboration aimed at reaching common ground to resolve conflict. Insight Mediation is transformative as the exploration of interpretation and meaning-making generates cognitive and physical insights that open new lines of curiosity and inquiry into conflicting parties' dialogue. These new understandings of what motivates each other's behaviour help parties communicate without judgement or aggression. It encourages them, with the mediator's support, to explore the values they are seeking to protect.

Dialogue produces new understandings of the conflict situation, as depicted in the illustration below (PIM 15). When parties realize they may have misunderstood each other, the sense of threat decreases helping them adopt a new attitude that opens the way to resolve their differences or live with them more peacefully.

Left pyramid:

Conflict

Defend patterns of interaction

Decision to defend (fight / flight)

Notice threat & its significance

Threat-based actions, words, non-verbal

Threats de-escalate through the use of curious questions about knowing, valuing, deciding

Right pyramid:

No Conflict

New patterns of interaction

Non-threatening responses discovered

New insights about knowing, valuing, deciding

Non-threat-based actions, words, gestures, non-verbal

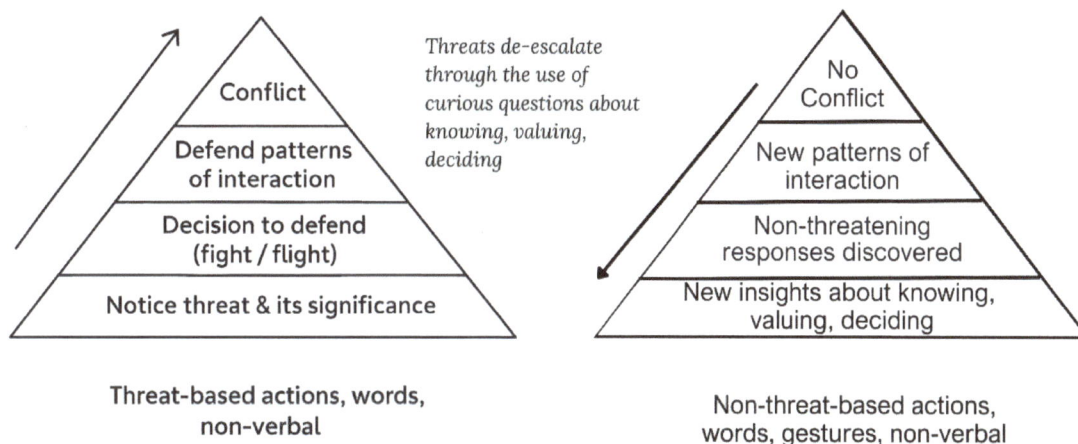

What Is the Learning Theory Behind Insight Mediation?

Learning in Insight Mediation involves more than the generation and passive reception of information. It is a complex non-linear and ongoing process that involves experiencing, understanding, verifying, valuing, deciding, and acting.

Aristotle argued individuals have an innate drive to understand their day-to day-world, and this drive is the foundation of learning, intellectual growth, and the philosophical quest to understand the world and our place within it. As Insight mediators we learn this innate drive manifests as a curiosity to ask questions to understand. And when our curiosity hits upon the answer to our questions, insights are produced: insights that are experienced in powerful and affective ways (PIM 36). Insight mediators know learning is a critical component of constructive dialogue and why the operations of learning are at the core of Insight Mediation.

What are Lonergan's Operations of Learning and how did they come to form the foundation of Insight Mediation?

Lonergan's five operations of learning help Insight mediators understand what happens in dialogue to bring about understanding:

1) Experiencing and Noticing.
2) Understanding and Insight.
3) Verifying Understanding.
4) Verifying Valuing.
5) Deciding and Acting.

These operations involve an ongoing process that helps answer questions about the everyday world. While questioning often goes unnoticed, insights occur when our curiosity discovers answers to our questions. In a mediation session the conflicting parties and mediator are learning thus engaged in the operations as depicted in the diagram below:

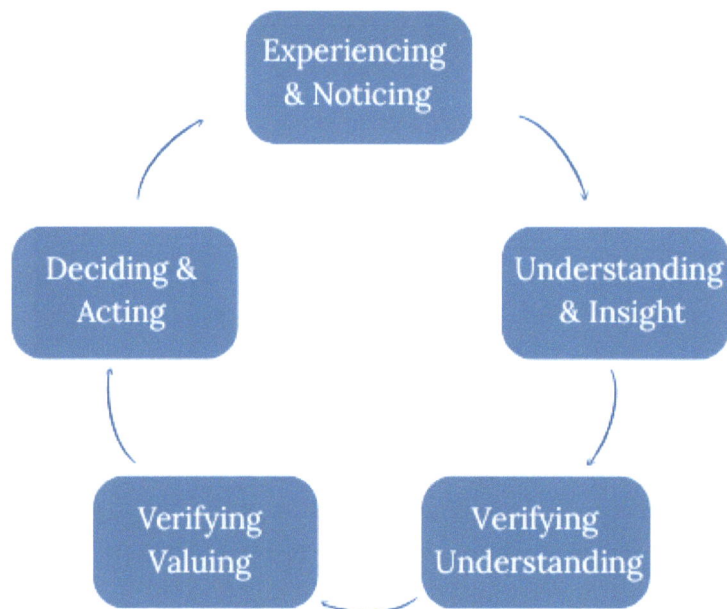

Let's look more closely at each operation.

The first operation, *Experiencing and Noticing,* immerses us in detecting and collecting data on the experiences of seeing, hearing, feeling, imagining and remembering- then questioning what we see, hear, feel, imagine and remember (PIM 38). In Insight Mediation this requires paying close attention to parties' actions, words and responses, and then engaging parties in experiential interactions that cultivate new forms of awareness. The core Insight skill 'noticing' helps the mediator achieve this. Yet, parties are seldom content merely experiencing as experiences evoke questioning.

The next operation, *Understanding and Insight,* involves the desire to make sense of others' actions and our own experiences, as experiencing is not the same as understanding. Understanding is when 'insight' occurs—insights that answer parties' questions (linking) or leads their questioning to a new path (de-linking). The desire to understand is about finding answers to questions such as: *What is it? What could this be? What does this mean?* Achieving insight is all about asking questions that open new lines of curiosity and inquiry. Becoming more curious about oneself in relation to others is at the heart of the learning process. This is why we refer to learning as the *operating system* of the Insight approach.

'Understanding arises when individuals learn something new about the reasons for their actions and reactions, and this new knowing opens the possibility of different choices.'

Following this, the operation of *Verifying Understanding* engages us in questions to determine *'do I have this right*?', given our insights can be wrong. The importance of ensuring correct understanding led to the creation of another core Insight skill, 'verifying'. This skill purposely leads to wondering and questioning: *Is what I now understand correct? Have I missed something important? Is there more to know*? This line of questioning brings us back to our own experience to look for evidence—either to confirm our insight or to guide us toward new ones.

The operation, *Verifying Valuing,* involves reflecting on why what we have learned about what matters—to ourselves and others—truly matters to us. We value, then verify we understand what is valued. *What is important here? What is important to me? What is important to others?* Our feelings come into play, and as we explore our feelings, we discover the values they evoke. Valuing involves examining our values and considering whether they are sufficient and reflect our best selves. Based on the significance of what we now know we ask *'so what*?' Learning is not a linear process, it involves looping back to experience, understanding and verifying with questions about values.

The final operation, *Deciding and Acting,* involves using our understanding and valuing to take—or choose not to take—responsibility for our actions. It seeks to answer 'so knowing what I now know, what will I do?'; we decide then act. It involves considering our options and whether we have the courage to act on them. It answers the questions, *How should I act? What is the best I can do, and will I do it?* The focus is on the best we will actually do, given what we have gained from performing the other operations. *Acting* is about doing what I decided to do based on the answers to the previous questions; *This is how I will act on my understanding.* We take a stand, become personally involved, and follow through with our decision to act.

As depicted in the diagram on the next page, the action we take generates a new experience, and the operations of learning cycle can begin again.

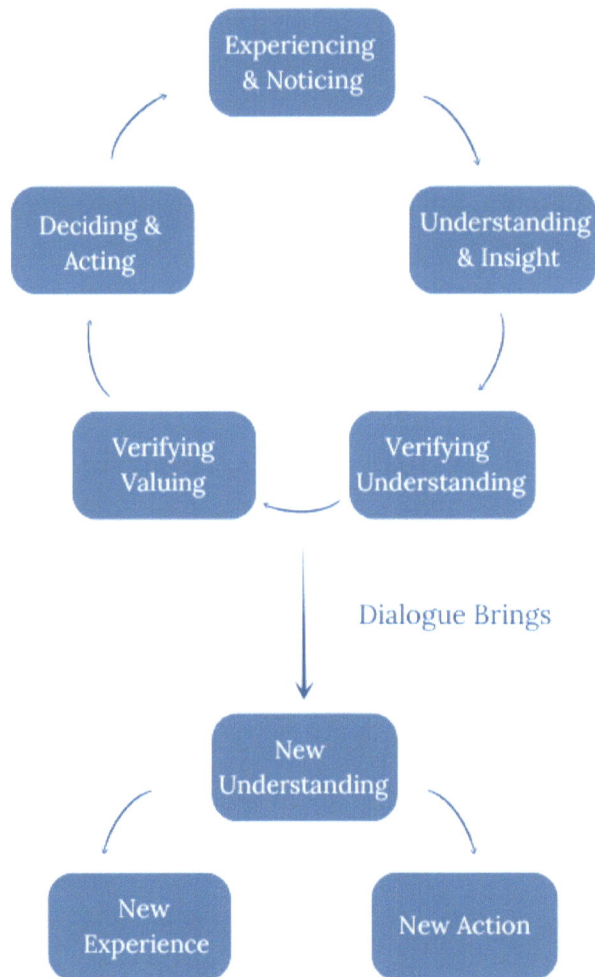

Understanding how Insight learning theory and the operations of learning shape an Insight mediator's actions is essential. As you move through this *Guide* notice your use of the operations of learning, and your ability to recognize these operations within yourself.

The '*Insight Mediator Self-assessment Tool*' in PIM, pages 177-179, was designed to help Insight mediators consider how effectively they are applying these ideas in their conflict work. You are encouraged to reflect on the questions asked in Appendix B. Validation of the power of these operations will emerge through the responses from parties you are working with – do your questions unblock learning and understanding? Or do parties continue articulating their defend stories?

In summary, Insight Mediation differs from approaches where the mediator helps parties find common ground or negotiate solutions. Instead, the Insight mediator's role is to help parties uncover the blocks caused by perceived threats that prevent them from understanding the deeper values their conflict behaviour is protecting. This requires they discover threats-to-cares, which involves asking curious questions about threats to help parties identify the cares they are protecting when they respond defensively. Once these blockages are identified and reduced, parties can often work independently—or with minimal guidance from the mediator—to find new solutions and make positive changes. As noted repeatedly, Insight Mediation is centered on learning. Parties learn about what is driving their actions and possible ways to change them, while mediators learn about what parties are experiencing, feeling and valuing. Through the mediation dialogue, parties reach a new understanding of themselves and each other. This new understanding leads to changed ways of interacting towards each other that generate a different experience of their relationship.

Summary of important Insight Mediation concepts that engage us in listening, learning and understanding:

- The Insight method is a non-linear, integrative, creative and emergent learning process that seeks to understand the cares parties are protecting.
- Insight mediators use learning theory to explain and change conflict behaviour.
- Interpretations of threat to deeply held values (cares) produce defend behaviours that block understanding between parties. Blocked understanding results in an absence of listening, curiosity and authentic questioning.
- Ongoing defend patterns of conflict behaviour create, sustain and escalate conflict by blocking curiosity and learning.
- New insights correct and expand what conflicting parties know, and this expanded understanding helps de-escalate threat, remove blocks to communication and alter conflict behaviour.
- Disrupting the certainty of knowing others as a threat helps produce curiosity, insights and learning.
- Insight mediators ask about interpretations of threat more than a party's intent. They notice, then ask about, defend responses and behaviours, and ensure the listener understands the speaker's meaning using the skill of 'listening to the listener.' They are also vigilant about noticing if parties' reactions to interactions are defensive as it means they interpreted them as judgemental and accusatory.
- Feeling threatened triggers defending conflict behaviours including arguing, resisting, explaining, re-explaining, escalated emotions, blaming others, denying responsibility, making excuses, bringing up past mistakes, using the silent treatment, gaslighting, attacking the person criticizing you, playing the victim, righteous indignation, and deflecting criticism by shifting focus to the other person's flaws.

Activities and Recommended Readings for Chapter 2

Noticing defend behaviours and strong feelings implores us to explore rather than suppress or side-step them; they tell us something of importance is being threatened. Become curious by wondering out loud and asking 'threat-based questions;' they are key to transforming the situation into one where parties become empowered to act towards each other in less threatening ways.

Learning is essential for achieving mutually satisfying agreements, which is why we must remain vigilant in ensuring that what we—and the parties—hear, interpret, and assume is accurate. This involves frequently confirming the accuracy of our 'knowing.' *This is what I am taking away from what you are saying, do I have this right?*

Activity 1: Asking threat-based, interpretative and verifying questions

Examples of threat-based questions include:

> *What concerns you most?*
>
> *What is threatening about this plan?*
>
> *What are the dangers of doing this now?*
>
> *What is making you so uneasy?*
>
> *What worries you about the draft plan?*
>
> *If you can't agree, what do you fear will happen / or not happen?*
>
> *You seem hesitant about her suggestion, talk about your doubts so we can better understand your reluctance. (example of bridging)*
>
> *Your averseness/unwillingness to look at this latest proposal is evident, what's holding you back from even being able to discuss it? (example of bridging)*
>
> *After noticing an eyeroll and look of exasperation you say: Her offer was clearly a 'no-go' suggestion, what is the worry if what she is asking happens?*

Practice: *Generate more threat-based questions and record them in your Learning Journal.*

Examples of Interpretive Questions include:

> *What are you hearing her say?*
>
> *When he does not reply, what is he telling you?*
>
> *What were you hoping for when you sent the email?*

How did you imagine meeting in person would help the situation?

You expected another reaction; what was your take-away on what was different?

What do you want her to know that you do not think she knows now?

From what was just said, what have you learned or understood?

How do you interpret that comment and what meaning do you ascribe to it?

How would you know if you made yourself understood?

Practice: *Generate more interpretive questions and record them in your Learning Journal.*

Examples of Verifying Questions:

Here is what I am taking from what you are saying…, do I have it right?

Jane is saying that she thinks you are in agreement, is that correct?

Share with us what you hear him saying about the arrangement, so he can let you know if you have it right?

Here is what I hear you asking him for; have I missed anything?

When you were talking, I thought about the issue you raised earlier about the summer schedule. Am I correct that they are related?

Is what the two of you are discussing now the central issue you disagree on?

At this point, you are happy with where we are and are in agreement on what happens next?

Practice: *Generate more verifying questions and record them in your Learning Journal.*

Activity 2. Listening to Understand

For each situation presented below: 1) restate the content, 2) reflect the emotion, and 3) provide a listening to understand response, which involves paraphrasing *both* content and emotion into one sentence. Here is an example:

'These mediation sessions always go overtime, and I can't continue to be away from the kids so much'.

Restate content: The mediation sessions often go overtime.

Reflect emotion: You are worried about being away from the kids.

Listening to Understand response: Being away from the kids when these mediation sessions go overtime worries you.

34

Restate content / Reflect emotion / Create a Listening to Understand response for each statement below and record them in your Learning Journal:

1. *I wish I was less taken for granted in this family; I have a lot to offer but feel so left out of things.*

2. *I prepared long and hard only to learn I was not invited to the discussions.*

3. *I made several suggestions to my parents, yet they paid no attention; it's as if I don't exist.*

RECOMMENDED READING

'*Four Distinguishing Features,*' Cheryl Picard and Kenneth Melchin (2022), Appendix D.

Take a moment to reflect on the four features of Insight Mediation that distinguish it from other mediation approaches. In your own words, summarize what the authors mean when they say, '*conflict is understood as arising from threats-to-cares.*' Write your answer in your Learning Journal.

NOTES

Chapter Three

THE INSIGHT MEDIATION METHOD

Dialogue is the most effective way of resolving conflict (Tenzin Gyatso, 14th Dalai Lama)

KEY TAKEAWAY

In conflict, experiences of threat trigger fight or flight responses that block parties from listening, learning and understanding. Learning through dialogue free of threat is key to resolving differences. Insight mediators provide a safe place for parties to discover they may be mistaken about the other's intentions. Learning begins when parties can let go of previous understanding enabling them to speak without judgement and defend-type behaviours and language. It is through learning parties discover they can choose to interact differently.

This chapter focuses on the method of Insight Mediation—an approach that is emergent, creative, and dynamic, continually responding to what is learned in the moment. Through this learning process, conflicting parties begin to recognize how their values, feelings assumptions, interpretations, and values shape their and others' behaviours. An Insight mediator uses this method to help parties move from threat-based misunderstanding to dialogue that expands awareness and generates insight revealing the feelings and values underlying their behaviour.

'Tell me and I forget, teach me and I may remember, involve me and I learn.' (Benjamin Franklin)

The Insight Mediation method includes five overlapping, non-linear phases that reveal the behaviours, fears, feelings, and values driving conflict when understanding is blocked. Transformation in conflict occurs when parties open their minds to genuine questioning and authentic curiosity about what truly matters to each other. Through this learning process, they discover and choose new ways of interacting.

Before exploring the five phases of Insight Mediation, it's important to consider preliminary steps to determine whether mediation should proceed. In this pre-mediation phase, the mediator assesses whether the process will be safe and fair for all. The mediator also clarifies the parties' expectations, addressing any misunderstandings about what mediation entails. Finally, the mediator—or whoever is responsible for convening—takes the necessary steps to prepare the parties and set the stage for a meaningful and constructive dialogue.

What happens before and after mediation?

The lead-up to mediation is known by several names. In workplace or community settings, it may be called pre-mediation, convening, or the preparation stage. In family mediation, it is often referred to as the intake process. In Insight Mediation, we typically use the term 'convening.' Whatever the terminology, this stage focuses on assessment, education and completing tasks outlined in legislation, organizational policy, or professional standards of practice. It is essential for mediators to follow the standards relevant to their field—for instance, family mediators must screen for intimate partner violence and power imbalances.

Holding separate sessions with each party before the first joint meeting is essential, as mediation is not always the most suitable dispute resolution option. Chapter 5 of PIM (104–112) outlines what occurs before and after Insight Mediation. Here, we briefly touch on these stages knowing they align closely with most mediation processes.

Pre-mediation may take place in person, by telephone, or virtually. The convenor—who may or may not be the mediator—requires strong communication skills and a solid understanding of mediation, other dispute-resolution methods, and relevant regulations. Their role includes ensuring that participation in mediation will not disadvantage the parties and, when mediation is not appropriate, guiding them toward alternative options. In Insight Mediation, pre-mediation goes beyond logistics and serves three key functions:

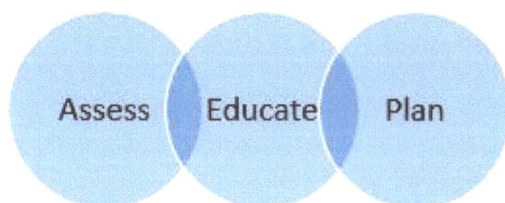

Assess   Educate   Plan

Assessing the Appropriateness of Mediation (PIM 107)

Below are examples of questions the mediator or convenor, is likely to ask parties about the nature of the dispute in order to begin assessing if participating in mediation would be appropriate, safe and fair.

> *What is the nature of the conflict you would like to resolve using mediation?*
>
> *How long has this been going on and what prompted it to come out in the open?*
>
> *How have the two of you typically handled conflict in the past?*

What is making it so difficult that you would like the help of a mediator?

Talk a bit about how the two of you interact when you are together.

How might a successful mediation make things better for you?

What, if any, special or accessibility needs do you have?

How open are you to discovering a different viewpoint about the situation?

Practice: *Think of questions to learn more about the situation and readiness of parties for mediation. Record these questions in your Learning Journal. For more examples, see pages 107-109 of PIM.*

Educating the Parties (PIM 108)

The convenor explains the mediation process so parties can make an informed decision about participating. This includes clarifying the process itself, as well as the roles of the mediator and the parties. These conversations also reveal how open—or resistant—each party may be to learning something new.

Have you ever been involved in mediation before? If yes, what was your experience?

Do you know anyone who has been to mediation? Based on what they told you, what are you expecting will happen?

What worries do you have about going to mediation?

Are there institutional policies or practices that impact your ability to make decisions on your own? Do decisions need to be ratified? Who do you need to consult with?

What would you like to know from me to help you feel confident to make an informed decision about moving forward with mediation?

Practice: *Record other questions you could ask to help educate the parties in your Learning Journal.*

Planning the Session and Coaching the Parties (PIM 109)

A convenor often helps parties prepare for mediation by coaching them on constructive ways to engage. Parties may be asked to reflect in advance on what they hope to achieve, what matters most to them, and how open they are to discovering they may have misinterpreted the other party's actions. Through this process, the convenor models curiosity and learning while exploring how each party feels about the possibility of mediation. When planning the mediation, the convenor also gathers key information by asking questions such as:

> *What has been happening that's made it difficult for you both to work through this on your own?*
>
> *What expectations do you have regarding time, location or other logistics?*
>
> *How soon can the first session be scheduled?*
>
> *How do you imagine decisions being finalized; in writing or verbally agreed upon?*
>
> *Think about how open you are to the possibility of learning you may be wrong about some things?*
>
> *If you plan to bring a lawyer, what role are you expecting they will take?*
>
> *Is there anyone else you want to bring, and how would that be helpful?*

Practice: *What additional questions would help plan a session and coach the parties? Record your answers in your Learning Journal.*

In Insight Mediation, the pre-mediation phase helps determine whether mediation should proceed and how to set it up for success. It includes coaching parties on what to expect, supported by written materials or videos when available. These sessions also reveal how open parties are to learning and to reconsidering unverified assumptions—such as believing the other's actions were meant to cause harm.

Beyond preparing for and facilitating mediation, Insight mediators commonly follow up with parties afterward (PIM 111). This follow-up serves two key purposes:

- checking in on how the parties are relating to each other and how they are managing the agreements made during mediation.
- gathering feedback on the parties' satisfaction with both the mediation process and the mediator. In some cases, this follow-up may include a formal evaluation of the mediation's outcomes and overall impact.

What is the method of Insight Mediation?

A key feature of Insight Mediation is helping parties understand when something they value feels threatened, their natural response is to defend. This defensive behaviour can be interpreted by others as a threat to what they value, prompting them to defend in return.

Conflict arises when these patterns of defensive responses block learning and reinforce limited assumptions about each other's intentions.

'Learning how our actions and the actions of others can create and sustain conflict provides insight on how we might respond differently in a similar situation in the future. Changing our actions can change how others act. Changes brought about through learning can be powerful and lasting.'

Insight Mediation provides conflicting parties the opportunity to discover a new understanding of what is going on. To do this the Insight mediator engages conflicting parties in a dialogue to explore and verify, *'is it necessarily so'* the other party's behaviour signals an attack, helping them see that their relationship need not remain defined by threat. To answer this question the Insight mediator assesses how open or blocked the parties are to learning about one another. This is followed by entering into a dialogue that expands what parties now know. Unblocking learning through mediation often reveals conflict behaviours are not only acts of intentional harm, but responses to feelings of threat to what parties care about or to protecting themselves against an unwelcome future.

Helping parties gain a new understanding of each other's behaviour generates new insights. It is these new understandings that produce the curiosity needed for parties to engage in dialogue about less threatening ways of interacting. Said another way, Insight Mediation is directed toward expanding information and correcting misunderstanding by disrupting the certainty of knowing each other *only* as a threat.

Transformation begins when parties open their minds to genuine questioning and authentic curiosity about each other's cares. In threat-free dialogue, real learning can occur. New understanding through leaning shifts parties' focus from 'what they want' to 'the values they are protecting,' allowing parties to see that they can choose to act differently. This emphasis on learning distinguishes Insight Mediation from approaches centered on resolving competing interests, unmet needs, or incompatible goals. For example, a father may realize that his ex-partner's insistence on a routine for the children stems not from control but from concern for their anxiety—a shift from judgement to curiosity, as in the following illustration:

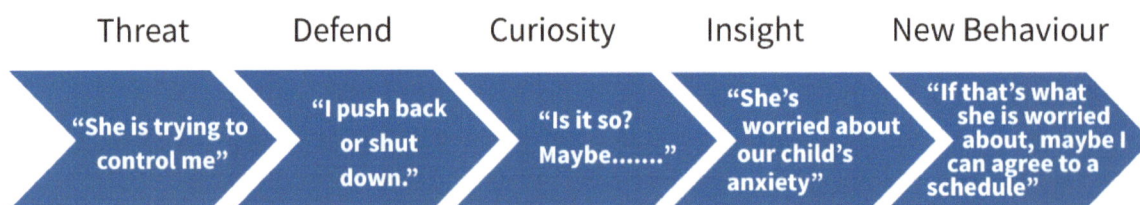

Threat	Defend	Curiosity	Insight	New Behaviour
"She is trying to control me"	"I push back or shut down."	"Is it so? Maybe……."	"She's worried about our child's anxiety"	"If that's what she is worried about, maybe I can agree to a schedule"

What are the Phases of Insight Mediation?

Facilitating 'learning conversations' that help parties discover new possibilities in their relationships unfold through five interconnected, non-linear, and dynamic phases, each with its own purpose and complexity.

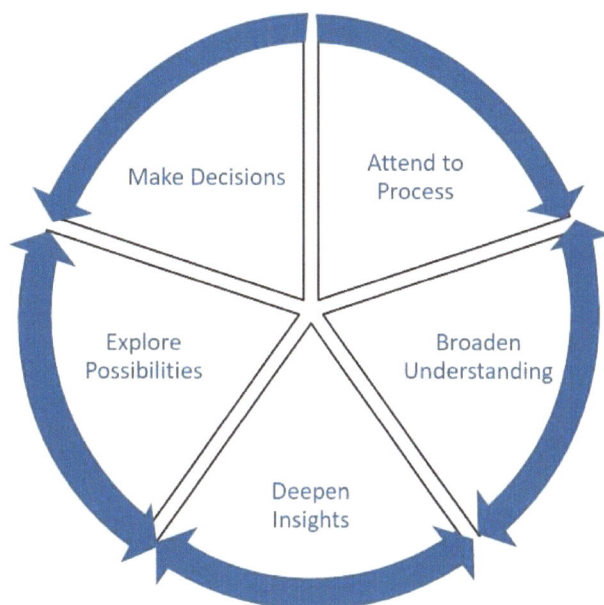

Phase 1: *Attend To Process*

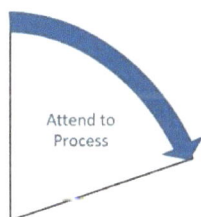

In Phase 1, (PIM 60-72). Insight mediators 'attend' to process by engaging parties from the start in a conversation that demonstrates the process will be shared by the parties and the mediator. This differs from models where the mediator begins by informing parties about what is going to happen. This distinction is deliberate. In contrast to models that want parties to know the mediator is the one in charge of the process, in Insight Mediation the message being communicated is that the mediator and the parties are co-responsible for how the mediation is undertaken. Attending to process, rather than introducing the process, is also viewed as creating and maintaining an environment that supports genuine curiosity and shared understanding.

In the first joint session, the Insight mediator focuses on building rapport and reinforcing that the parties control what is discussed and decided. The mediator's style, confidence, and ability to listen non-judgementally are communicated through their interactions, helping reduce anticipated threats and heightened emotions. Skillfully addressing parties' questions and concerns in a curious, confident and balanced manner further establishes a safe space for learning to take place.

Other Phase 1 tasks involve:

- Reviewing the *Consent to Mediate* form (PIM 171-172) and having parties sign it ensures they share a common understanding of the process and demonstrates their commitment to seriously attempt to resolve their differences.

- Facilitating an interactive discussion with the parties about their role by asking them how they see their responsibilities; what they need from each other; and what they need from you as mediator to create a safe learning environment.

- Reviewing your role as mediator, assuring parties you will be curious, attentive and responsive, impartial and non-judgemental, while emphasizing outcome decisions remain entirely with them.

- Engaging the parties in an interactive discussion about confidentiality, session timeframes, the possibility of caucusing, and other protocols, rather than simply setting ground rules.

- Being transparent about creating a fair and safe environment and reassuring parties they are supported in resolving their differences. Being elicitive, transparent and interactive about process may sound like this:

> *What do you need from me, and each other, to feel safe sharing all that needs to be said so this mediation can be successful?*
>
> *I will listen carefully and verify my understanding of what you say, and ensure each of you accurately hears the other. To do this, I will ask the listener to share what they understood, then confirm with the speaker that it reflects their intended meaning.*

Before concluding this phase, the mediator will discuss expectations for the end of mediation. This includes decisions about confidentiality in reporting, both verbal and written, and clarifying whether the mediator will draft 'Progress Notes' for use between sessions or final documents such as 'Mediation Reports,' 'Memorandums of Understanding,' or 'Outcome Agreements' (PIM 173–175). The mediator also addresses whether legal or other forms of ratification will be required before any outcome documents are signed.

Each party is asked to confirm their understanding of the process and readiness to begin. Once confirmed, the mediator proceeds to Phase 2: Broaden Understanding.

Practice: *Review PIM 60-72 and create a 'cheat sheet' of what to talk about in Phase 1. Add this list to your Learning Journal.*

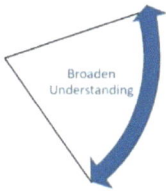

Phase 2: *Broaden Understanding*

In Phase 2 (PIM 72-79) the mediator asks broad open-ended questions about each party's hopes for a better tomorrow as a way to begin surfacing the threats underlying the parties' conflict behaviours. This is in contrast to models that begin by gathering facts about problem issues and behaviours through parties' opening statements. The point of moving away from more traditional opening statements is they often contain positional and entitled defend arguments about being right. When a listening party hears a speaker's opening statement as a challenge to their views and claims, it further blocks their ability to listen and learn making it even more difficult for the mediator to facilitate a productive dialogue. Recognizing this drawback, Insight Mediation pioneers came up with a strategy that came to be known as 'asking the hope question' (PIM 73; Appendix E); a question aimed at surfacing what is behind parties' decision to use mediation. Said another way, it tries to make known what parties hope will *improve* for them rather than what they *want*.

Opening the mediation by exploring each party's hopes for a better tomorrow helps reveal the 'valuing' beneath the hope. Asking, '*What are you hoping will be better in your life tomorrow if you can talk about what matters to you today?*' helps the mediator guide the parties toward a less defensive, more insightful dialogue. This focus on hopes for a positive future is a distinctive feature of Insight Mediation.

In the Insight approach, conflict emerges from the experience that one party's actions pose a threat to another's deeply held values. This experience triggers a defensive response that blocks learning and understanding.

Let's deepen on this. At this early stage, argumentative dialogue can heighten existing emotions and perceptions of threat, which in turn escalates conflict behaviours. Asking about the hopes that brought parties to mediation reveals the 'big picture motive' behind their participation—a motive rooted in care rather than demand. This is especially relevant because parties often enter mediation prepared to defend their position and assert what they want, aiming to convince the mediator they are right and should prevail. In these truncated states parties often struggle to express a genuine hope rather than a disguised demand, even after pre-mediation preparation. The hope question is powerful because it does more than surface a hope; it provides direction from the parties themselves for the mediator to begin exploring the value-based narratives underlying the conflict.

It is important to emphasize asking the hope question involves asking a *series* of layered relational questions. The goal is to elicit new and less threat-producing information the mediator can use to guide Phase 3 exploration. This process helps parties open their minds, allowing genuine questioning and authentic curiosity to emerge. Below are two examples of hope questions.

> *What are you hoping will be better for you and for the Team when you return to work if you are able to talk to each other today about what is most concerning to all of you?*
>
> *How do you hope relations will improve between you if you are able to have a full and honest conversation about this situation that is so worrisome?*

Practice: *Review PIM 73 about the power of hopes, then write your own examples of hope questions in your Learning Journal.*

As noted earlier, parties often enter mediation ready to defend their positions. Shifting the focus to their hopes, rooted in what they care about, requires the mediator to ask a series of layered, relational questions. The working paper *'Setting a Strong Foundation for a Learning Conversation'* (Appendix E) explores this in more detail through an intergenerational mediation. The excerpt below from this working paper illustrates asking the hope question.

> The mediator asks Carla to talk about her hopes for a better tomorrow to which she blurts:
>
> *I just want Adrianna to do what is best and right for our mom and stop being so selfish!*
>
> The mediator then asks a question that follows from this answer:
>
> *You want what's best for your mom. And if Adrianna were to do what you think is best for your mom, how would this make tomorrow better for you?*
>
> With exasperation Carla answers:
>
> *Well for one thing, mom would not be alone and then I wouldn't have to worry all the time about her falling and hurting herself!*
>
> The mediator asks a layered question that follows from Carla's answer to the question before:
>
> *You are very worried about your mother's safety and you don't want to worry all the time. You're hoping that this conversation will make things better for you in what way?*
>
> Carla responds,

Well, I wouldn't have to call and check up on her three times a day or wonder why she hasn't called me back. I'd be able to focus on my own life and deal with my own problems for a change.

The mediator uses this information to note a learning conversation may be possible between the two sisters when their sense of threat is sufficiently diminished:

One of the conversations you are hoping to have with Adrianna today involves how to ensure mom is safe from harm. And that would give you greater peace of mind so you can focus more on your own life. I've made a note for us to come back to that at some point. Before we do, it is important we hear from Adrianna about what her hopes are for a better tomorrow if we can talk about what matters to her today.

Mediators with different training may ask questions about hopes or reasons for coming to mediation with intentions that differ from those of an Insight mediator. Mediators focused on identifying negotiable interests might ask about hopes to find entry points for negotiation. In contrast, an Insight mediator asks about hopes to spark curiosity and foster learning as a pathway to begin searching for potential change. The hope question helps shift a party's focus away from the certainty of threat that drives their 'defend story.' (PIM 28).

Even after eliciting parties' hopes for a better tomorrow, Insight pioneers observed parties often continued to defend themselves or blame the other. They also noticed that exploring these stories tended to escalate the other party's defensive behaviours, and the longer this continued, the more difficult the interactions became. Recognizing this as problematic, they labeled it a 'defend story.' To guide Insight mediators beyond the defend story, they developed the concept of the 'threat-to-care story.' This story holds what truly matters to a party and explains what they are defending and why. Distinctions between these two types of stories are outlined below.

Differentiating a Defend Story from a Threat-to-Care Story

DEFEND STORIES

- My rationale for being right & knowing other as wrong
- Closed with no room for change due to certainty of knowing my actions are justified
- Constructed from assumptions, interpretations & feelings about conflict events and behaviours
- Firmly held interpretations embedded in identity; story is rejected by other party
- Fuels the conflict & keeps it ongoing

THREAT-TO-CARES STORY

- Express meaning-making & significance related to sense of threat; surfaces cares
- Explain how what matters (cares) is experienced as threats in need of protection
- Rarely shared & seldom heard by others
- Hold potential for parties to re-interpret each other's intentions & actions through new understandings that alter behaviours
- Opens pathway for change

Surfacing parties' 'threat-to-care stories' is an Insight strategy in which the mediator temporarily sets aside the content of a party's defend narrative. While some details from the defend story may be addressed later in Phase 4, *Exploring Possibilities*, and Phase 5, *Making Decisions*, the immediate focus is helping the party identify the values at stake. This approach shifts curiosity toward what parties do not yet understand about each other, rather than defending what they think they already know, preventing escalation of defensive behaviours.

Phase 2 is relatively brief, as the mediator's main focus is surfacing potential avenues to reduce defensive behaviours. At this stage, the mediator does not explore underlying threats or cares in depth. By uncovering hopeful narratives through the hope question, the mediator discovers ways to begin shifting the dialogue from patterns of 'attack' to explorations of cares, transitioning from the *Broadening Understanding* to the *Deepen Insights* phase.

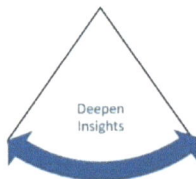

Phase 3: *Deepen Insights*

The *Deepen Insights* phase (PIM 79–93) focuses on uncovering and exploring the threats driving parties' behaviour. When parties feel threatened, their thinking becomes constricted, blocking listening, learning and understanding. With this in mind, the mediator closely observes parties' feelings, as they reflect the values underlying their words and actions (PIM 44). They focus on creating learning opportunities by expanding information and verifying understanding. The *Deepen Insights* phase lies at the heart of Insight Mediation and is where much of the 'magic' happens. Furthermore, in this phase an observer would notice an Insight mediator begin to slow the dialogue by taking time to deepen understanding and generate curiosity about the threats-to-cares surfaced in Phase 2. We can see this in the mediator's intervention below:

> *It made sense to you, Sally, to go over John's head and talk to the manager when you thought he was intentionally handing his reports in late to make you look bad. Your worry was bolstered by the number of recent layoffs, and you became fearful of losing your job. As a single parent with young children losing your job would be very difficult, and you needed to prevent this from happening.*

The dialogue above exemplifies what Insight mediators mean by 'disrupting the certainty of parties knowing each other only as a threat.' This central idea is captured in the core principle of Insight Mediation practice:

> *Conflict emerges when individuals or groups experience threats to their desires and needs, expected patterns of cooperation, or deeply held judgements about social order that lead them to respond defensively. Defend*

responses feel like threats to others and they too respond defensively, creating defend patterns of interaction that sustain the conflict. Through deepening conversations, a mediator assists parties to gain insights that produce new understandings and alter defend patterns of interaction so that learning and change can occur (PIM 80).

In Insight Mediation, 'noticing' is a core skill. Here is an example:

When the mediator notices parties' responses remain accusatory and lacking in curiosity it indicates parties are still feeling threatened and protecting what matters to them; learning has not yet become unblocked. Noticing this, the mediator is likely to suggest slowing the conversation and reviewing the discussion to ensure parties are accurately hearing and understanding each other. To do this the mediator can employ the skill of 'listening to the listener' (PIM 22). This involves asking the listener to restate what they heard from the speaker. If the listener struggles or cannot accurately convey the speaker's message, it indicates learning is still blocked, and continuing the dialogue would be unproductive, requiring a different strategy. A typical 'listening to the listener' exchange might sound like:

> *'Sally has been telling you some of the reasons she went to your supervisor, what did you hear her say about why that happened?' Or, 'What meaning are you attaching to her not coming to talk to you first?'*

Practice: *Review PIM 22 and create your own examples of listening to the listener questions in your Learning Journal.*

In Phase 3, you will notice an Insight mediator asking 'layered questions' (PIM 129 & 134) to explore and deepen parties' threat-to-care stories. At the same time, the mediator avoids delving into a party's defend story, focusing instead on the care they are protecting. This might sound like:

> *'Clearly you are worried if you do not stop this from happening something bad will happen; what is that something bad?'*

You will also notice the Insight mediator closely observes when parties begin speaking directly to each other. At that point, the mediator takes a step back yet continuing to listen, speaking less while monitoring for shifts from curious dialogue back to defensive behaviour. If this occurs, the mediator practices 'transparency' (PIM 134–135) by sharing observations and asking, with genuine curiosity, what triggered the feeling of threat and defensive behaviour.

Practice: *Review PIM 129 and 134 and provide examples of layered questions in your Learning Journal.*

An Insight mediator uses the strategy of 'deepening the learning conversation' (PIM 43, 79, 132–134) to explore specific threats-to-care or feelings driving a party's conflict behaviour. This approach employs skills such as bridging, layered questions, linking and delinking, and finishing and using. Deepening the conversation might sound like this:

> *Sally, it is clear that you feel strongly about not adhering to the schedule and not wavering from it. What is your worry if changes were to be made?*
>
> *How would you know if what you are worried about were to be happening? What would you be noticing?*
>
> *And if you were to notice that, how could you approach John knowing what you now know so he doesn't feel you are' hanging him out to dry' as he did this last time?*

Deepening the learning conversation benefits parties since it expands their current knowing. This happens when the mediator provides a safe space for parties to discover they may have been, or are wrong, about the other's intentions. This new understanding encourages parties to speak and listen in a way *not* charged with judgement or blame, thus allowing genuine curiosity to surface and understanding to emerge. As learning expands parties discover they can choose to do things differently.

'When parties discover how each other's present behaviour is linked to feelings from the past and projected onto the future, they can begin to make sense of each other's actions, about which they were only able to make unfounded assumptions.'

Insight mediators use a strategy called 'linking' (PIM 140–142) to explore how threats-to-cares relate to parties' current behaviours and demands. Recognizing that actions and positions often stem from past experiences or anticipated negative futures, linking uncovers how these past and imagined threats drive present conflict. The diagram on the next page illustrates how present behaviours connect to past events and expected future outcomes.

Linking Present to Past and Future

PAST EXPERIENCE — Emotions, Beliefs, Culture
PRESENT BEHAVIOUR — Attitudes, Defend Responses, Feelings
FUTURE EXPECTATIONS — Fear of Future Dire Events

Two additional key strategies in the Insight method are 'Exploring Expected Futures,' detailed in Appendix F, and 'What the Insight Mediator Is Looking For,' outlined in Appendix E.

In the working paper *'Exploring Expected Futures,'* the authors explain this strategy is important when parties are stuck in defend behaviours and unable to listen or understand each other. Perceived threats are blocking listening, learning and understanding. The Insight mediator responds by shifting focus away from repetitive defend stories and asking curious, non-judgemental questions about the cares each party is protecting and the unwanted or feared futures they are trying to avoid. These questions generate new insights, often prompting parties to reconsider their assumptions about the other's intentions. This approach, combined with the safe space created by the mediator, allows parties to listen without feeling threat. By asking about each party's hopes, cares, threats, and imagined futures in relation to their own experience, the mediator ensures the conversation focuses on the speaker's perspective, not the listener, thus avoiding blame or accusation.

After verifying the listener's understanding of what the speaker said is correct, a similar exploration occurs with the other party about their hopes, cares and threats in relation to their expected future. Engaging in listening, learning and understanding without the experience of threat frees parties from defending, thereby allowing them to listen, learn and understand outside of mediation. The following questions exemplify asking about threat and cares in relation to one's own experience and expected future.

> *Clearly there is something still troubling you about what he is offering to do as a way to resolve the situation, what are you worried will happen if his suggestions do not work?*

There is something important to you about being sure the payments will arrive on time that you are trying hard to protect. What are you trying to prevent from happening?

You have repeated that point several times now, and that tells me that you are imagining something worrying will happen if this does not go forward exactly as discussed. What worries you about taking the additional time she is requesting that you want to avoid happening?

Practice: *Create additional questions that ask parties about their expected futures and record them in your Learning Journal.*

What is the Insight Mediator looking for?

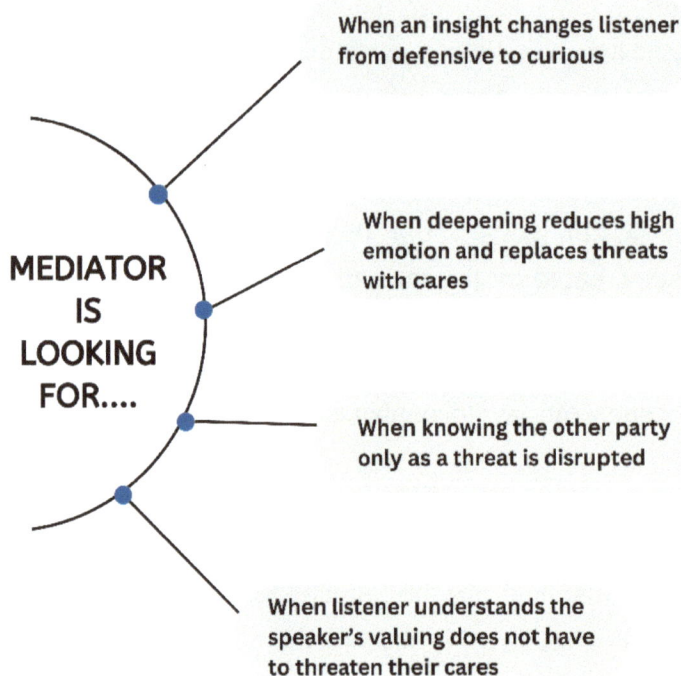

MEDIATOR IS LOOKING FOR....

- When an insight changes listener from defensive to curious
- When deepening reduces high emotion and replaces threats with cares
- When knowing the other party only as a threat is disrupted
- When listener understands the speaker's valuing does not have to threaten their cares

First, Insight mediators pay close attention to when the listening party gains an insight that shifts their pattern of listening. For example, curiosity that leads one party to ask questions and the other to respond openly signals a reduction in perceived threat. Conversely, non-verbal cues indicating rising defensiveness show listening is blocked. Trained to notice these responses, the Insight mediator intervenes when conversations begin to revert to attack-defend patterns.

An example of an 'in-the-moment' interjection might sound like this:

I notice you have reverted to blaming her for what happened and that tells me you are feeling attacked in some way. Let's take a breath, think about what just happened and how you are feeling, and then I will ask each of you to share your thoughts as a way to get back to a more curious footing.

Second, Insight mediators focus on identifying and exploring feelings of threat, recognizing these feelings shape how parties respond and behave toward each other. Rather than merely naming or acknowledging emotions, mediators probe to understand the underlying values the feelings reflect. This is crucial because feelings point to values (PIM 44) and play a central role in creating and resolving conflict. Moreover, similar feelings can arise from different values for different parties, making it essential to explore what each party's feelings are truly about—an essential part of an Insight mediator's work.

Third, the mediator's own mental map—their internal framework shaped by experience, perception, memory, and emotion—enables them to notice when the listener shifts. Key changes occur when the listener begins to question their prior understanding of the speaker, recognizing they may have been mistaken. This awareness reawakens curiosity, creating space for new information and understanding. As a result, parties can generate fresh ideas for interacting in less threatening and defensive ways.

'Learning how values influence decisions empowers the parties to make different decisions by delinking threats through a three-step process of: 1) gaining insight into what we and others really care about (a direct insight), 2) realizing that prior assumptions about the other party's motivations are wrong (a reverse insight); and 3) evoking a new line of curiosity about others and their relationship to us.'

Fourth, when the listener recognizes the speaker's actions were not intended to harm what is important to them, it shows the mediator has successfully created a safe space for listening—this is the essence of 'what the Insight mediator is looking *for.*' This indicates the listener has de-linked, recognizing the care the speaker is protecting does not necessarily threaten their own important values. De-linking the perceived threat alters a party's interaction, as they no longer feel compelled to defend and can communicate without judgement or attack. When this shift occurs, the mediator can explore the value the party is protecting. As the listener opens their mind and engages in genuine questioning with authentic curiosity about the speaker's values, transformation occurs. It is in this threat-free dialogue that true understanding and real learning emerge.

Once parties no longer feel compelled to defend—having gained a clearer, less threatening understanding of each other and a better sense of what matters to them—they can shift their focus to finding ways to change the situation. This marks the beginning of Phase 4: Explore Possibilities.

Phase 4: *Explore Possibilities*

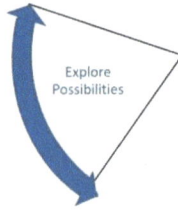

Phase 4 (PIM 93-99) guides parties to envision new ways of engaging with each other. This becomes possible through the earlier dialogue, which generated insights and shifted interactions from defensive to constructive. The focus now moves from understanding what matters to each other to exploring how, with this knowledge, they can act differently together.

Unlike some conflict approaches that focus on compromise or settling for less, this phase emphasizes creating solutions where parties' perspectives can coexist without threat. By fostering collaborative decision-making, it enables transformative outcomes that strengthen relationships and support constructive interactions both now and in the future.

The principle of self-determination is central to Insight Mediation. Decisions reached through the process are voluntary, made with full disclosure, and free from undue pressure to decide immediately. Transitioning into this phase often begins with the mediator summarizing the potential options suggested by the parties so far, followed by curious questions designed to generate an expanded list of possibilities.

> *'How about if I summarize the ideas already suggested as possible options, and then we can begin talking about additional possibilities. For now, we will just list them, later we will go through each one and talk in a more focused way about the pros and cons.'*
>
> *'Given what you have learned about what is of value to each of you and needs to be protected, what possibilities can you think of for moving forward? For now, we will just jot them down (brainstorm) without any discussion, later when no more ideas occur, we will examine them closely and eliminate those you know would not work.'*
>
> *'Given what you have learned about each other's worries, I'm wondering if this is the time to shift the conversation and talk about what doing things in a less-threatening way might look like.'*

Brainstorming without judgement is used to help parties expand their thinking about possible future actions. Once ideas have been exhausted, the mediator facilitates a discussion about which options are acceptable. Those that meet this standard are then examined more closely, including a 'reality check' to assess how feasible it would be to implement and follow through on them.

> *'It seems to me what you are agreeing to do is... How possible is it for that to happen in the timeframe you are looking at?'*

> *'You are offering something that would impact others in the group, do you have the authority to make that kind of decision today?'*
>
> *'How workable would that suggestion be given what we heard about everyone's very busy schedules?'*

| **Practice:** *Create a list of brainstorming and reality check questions in your Learning Journal.*

Sometimes the mediator may choose to carry a single concern through to exploring possible solutions rather than waiting for all issues to be identified. This approach is common in family or other long-standing, deep-rooted conflicts. Guiding the dialogue on one issue through to potential decision-making exemplifies the Insight mediator strategy of 'finishing' (PIM 137-138). Once one issue is addressed, the mediator returns to Phase 3 to engage in dialogue on other outstanding areas of disagreement.

During Phase 4, parties may sometimes slip back into defensive responses if they perceive the other as being accusatory or judgemental. The Insight mediator carefully watches for this and addresses it in the moment. Returning to productive dialogue is often straightforward, as most parties genuinely want to resolve their dispute—conflict is rarely enjoyable. When defensiveness arises, the mediator may respond with attentive listening followed by a curious question, a skill known as 'bridging' (PIM 139).

Bridging is powerful because it shows the mediator is both listening and genuinely engaged.

> *'I'm noticing Sally's suggestion brought out a defensive reaction John; how did you interpret Sally's intention in her suggestion that triggered your response?'*
>
> *'That request sparked an outburst from you Sally; what was your takeaway from what John is asking?'*

| **Practice**: *Have a look at PIM 139 and write some bridging questions in your Learning Journal.*

Parties may wish to discuss the options they are considering with others before making a final decision. Some may be required, or simply prefer, to seek legal advice before signing any agreements. In these situations, the mediator can create a list of the potential options and provide it to the parties, ensuring they do not have to rely on memory during their consultations.

Phase 5: *Making Decisions*

The final phase of Insight Mediation, 'Making Decisions,' occurs once parties have explored their concerns, questioned assumptions, broadened, and deepened their understanding of each other's feelings and cares. At this stage, they focus on articulating and choosing concrete actions. The mediator helps clarify the who, what, when, and where of the plan, ensuring decisions are informed and thoughtful. This phase emphasizes aligning actions with parties' insights, values, relationships, and future well-being.

Here, the mediator asks parties to reflect on the durability and satisfaction of the actions being considered and how their choices align with their new understanding of the conflict dynamics. The mediator does not make decisions; all outcomes are consensual and crafted by the parties themselves. Acting impartially, the mediator ensures parties leave with a clear understanding of how to engage constructively with one another.

'It is still a bit startling to me that, at this phase, when tensions have dissipated and planning for change is progressing well, it often happens that there is almost always something that has been misunderstood when agreements are being reviewed. Finding that out now helps to avoid problems in the future.'

Phase 5 emphasizes verifying understanding in detail. The mediator conducts a 'reality check' to confirm each party fully comprehends what has been agreed to. Misunderstandings are common, as assumptions and interpretations often obscure shared understanding. This step is critical: parties may feel relief the conflict is easing and assume they are aligned, but verification ensures clarity and agreement, preventing future miscommunication.

Once verification is complete, the mediator reviews how the agreed-upon outcomes will be documented or reported. Respecting that outcome decisions belong entirely to the parties, the conclusion of mediation can range from a simple handshake to a formal written agreement. The emphasis is on thoughtful, insight-driven resolutions rather than rushed compromises, reinforcing the transformative approach central to Insight Mediation.

Draft reports may be used to document decisions. While not final contracts, they capture key insights, shifts in perspective, and potential pathways forward, ensuring parties share a clear understanding of what was explored and decided during mediation. These reports summarize concerns, agreements, short and long-term actions, and any areas requiring further reflection. They serve as a tool to support informed decision-making, allowing participants to review and refine their understanding before making final commitments.

In addition to reviewing the actions parties will take to resolve their differences, the mediator discusses and verifies what will happen if the agreement breaks down or if earlier decisions need to be revised.

In organizational, workplace, or legal contexts, or when a third party is funding the mediation, it is common for the mediator to provide a report to the referring party. This may be done in writing, by phone, or in person. Regardless of the method, the mediator rarely discloses the content of the discussions; they only confirm that the mediation occurred and whether it was successful. Any reporting requirements are clearly outlined, explained, and agreed upon by all parties prior to the start of mediation.

The format of 'Outcome Agreements' can vary depending on the context. Agreements that require legal ratification or must comply with organizational policies are typically more formal and structured. In contrast, agreements arising from interpersonal or small-group disputes are usually less formal and written in plain, accessible language. A sample of a less formal outcome agreement, reflective of those commonly used in workplaces, churches, and similar settings, may be found in PIM 173–175.

This final phase of Insight Mediation is often personal and flexible reflecting the mediator's style or customary rituals. This may include activities such as shaking hands, using special pens to sign agreements, or other culturally appropriate gestures that acknowledge and celebrate the parties' efforts and accomplishments. For mediators bound by professional standards—for example, family mediators—there may be formal requirements for finalizing agreements, which can limit the use of informal rituals alone.

Activities and Recommended Readings for Chapter Three

Activity 1

Practice asking hope questions with a partner, or with friends or family. Ask them for feedback on how they experienced it.

Activity 2

Imagine you are teaching someone about the difference between a threat story and a defend story. How would you explain the difference?

Activity 3

The concept of mediator 'neutrality' is thought to be unrealistic given individuals have preferences and unconscious biases that emerge from their cultural and social backgrounds. Thus, by their very presence in a mediation they can alter the situation (PIM 59).   What are your thoughts on this?

Recommended Readings

It is recommended you read (re-read) the three (3) readings listed below as they speak strongly about the Insight Mediation method. After reading each paper, write the insights, questions or other highlights you took away from the papers in your Learning Journal

Setting a strong foundation for a learning conversation in Insight Mediation: The power of asking about hopes for an imagined better future' by Cheryl Picard and Marnie Jull, September 2023 Appendix C.

Exploring Expected Futures, Cheryl Picard, and Kenneth Melchin, 2023 Appendix F.

What is the Insight mediator looking for? by Kenneth Melchin, Cheryl Picard, and Mike Stebbins, 2023 Appendix E.

NOTES

Chapter Four

THE VALUE OF INSIGHT MEDIATORS LEARNING MORE ABOUT THEMSELVES IN RELATION TO OTHERS

To thine own self be true (William Shakespeare, *Hamlet*)

KEY TAKEAWAY

Foundational to the work of an Insight mediator is being aware of yourself in relation to others. Understanding yourself provides you with a heightened sense of how to help those in conflict discover their threats and underlying cares. Helping parties learn more about their own and others' threats-to-cares removes blocks to understanding.

Why is understanding yourself important to your work as a mediator?

The previous chapters explored what Insight mediators do. This chapter turns inward, examining how your personal worldview shapes your actions. Understanding how you make meaning of everyday experiences is essential to effective mediation.

Paying attention to yourself in conflict situations helps you recognize threat-based patterns of behaviour in both yourself and others. Understanding what you care about—and how those values are linked to your actions—offers insight into how parties may connect their behaviours to the protection of their own cares. The 'Learning Journal' introduced at the start of this Guide, along with the guidance in Appendix A, is designed to support your growth in self-awareness and personal understanding.

'Knowing yourself is the beginning of all wisdom'
(Aristotle)

Insight practitioners rely on self-knowledge and draw confidence from a strong theoretical framework that guides them to notice, value, and make thoughtful decisions throughout a dynamic learning journey with conflicting parties. Personal and professional growth, the exploration of relationships, skill development, and creative, emergent design are hallmarks of this practice—inviting Insight mediators into a continuous process of learning with themselves and the parties they serve. Intentionally examining your assumptions and interpretations through Lonergan's guiding question—'Is it so?'—creates the checks and balances needed for genuine change and transformation—for yourself and others. This is the focus of Chapter Four. Let's explore how this process unfolds.

What role does communication play in understanding more about ourselves?

As you reflect on yourself in conflict, consider how you communicate in these moments. Because people constantly interpret words and nonverbal cues—body language, actions, even silence—it is essential to notice and verify interpretations you make about what you see and hear. This involves confirming you and others have accurately received the message to ensure clear communication. Accurate meaning-making, correct interpretations, and verified assumptions lay the groundwork for resolving conflict effectively. Reflecting on your communication patterns—in conflict and in mediation—helps you grow as a mediator.

> *Do I talk more than listen?*
>
> *Do I give answers more than ask questions?*
>
> *Do I try to 'put the lid' on strong statements or high emotions?*
>
> *How comfortable am I with uncertainty? With silence? With disagreement? With anger?*

Awareness of your answers to the questions above provides valuable insight into your strengths and challenges when faced with conflict, along with those you are helping deal with conflict.

Understanding ourselves in relation to others is a dynamic process—the more you know the more you stand to change. In *Coming to our Senses: Healing Ourselves and the World through Mindfulness*, p. 237 (2005), Jon Kabat-Zinn suggests the only time we have to learn, or change, or grow is the present. Gaining a better understanding of the conflict experience revealed through communication patterns and emotions helps surface the cares being threatened. Realizing feelings carry values means you need to reflect on your valuing, otherwise it may go unnoticed.

Feelings play a central role in conflict, which is why it's important to surface and explore your own. By noticing, acknowledging, and normalizing your emotions—and asking yourself curious, reflective questions—you can uncover what you care about and what may feel threatened. In an online post Lang (2018) suggests elicited questions '...*nurture self-reflection and assist parties to explore the nature, history and impact of their conflict and that these questions encourage curiosity.*'

Insight theory is useful here as it teaches individuals experience 3 interconnected hierarchical levels of value (PIM 44):

1) *Personal:* (things we desire and need at the individual level)

2) *Relational:* (expected and cooperative patterns of relations we depend on to meet the needs of ourselves *and* others)

3) Social*:* (critical assessment of level 2 needs about justice, human rights and other unfair social structures and practices).

Identifying which level(s) of value undergird experiences of threat in conflict is critical to discovering less conflictual and lasting ways of interacting. And, as discussed in previous chapters, knowing feelings are connected to past experiences and imagined futures that hold unwelcome consequences opens a vista of self-exploration you may not have explored until now. In addition, increasing your awareness of your conflict style and personality traits can help you better understand your 'knee-jerk' conflict reactions, and provide you with promising options for more successful interactions and resolutions.

How does knowing more about conflict styles and personality traits help you notice your own responses to conflict?

Paying attention to your conflict emotions and behaviours engages you in discovery about what 'pushes your buttons' and your commonplace 'knee-jerk reaction' when they are pushed. Becoming a self-reflective practitioner involves querying the origins of your conflict reactions and behaviours.

One way to do this is to reflect on an early experience of conflict and ask yourself what you learned about conflict from your family of origin. Were you encouraged to express yourself openly when angry, confused, cross, or grumpy? Or were you silenced, or shamed in some way? What cues told you which behaviour was acceptable, and which was not?

By recognizing your own patterns in conflict, you strengthen your ability as a mediator to observe and explore how parties experience and respond to their situations. Since each person is unique, it is important not to assume that their actions have the same meaning as they would if performed by you or someone else. Being mindful of your cares and perspectives on conflict deepens your understanding of your responses and reveals patterns in others, guiding your further exploration.

To build self-knowledge, mediation trainers often ask participants to reflect on their typical conflict behaviours. One widely used tool is the Thomas–Kilmann Conflict Mode Instrument (TKI) first published in 1974, which measures responses along two dimensions: assertiveness and cooperativeness. These dimensions define five approaches to conflict: avoiding, competing, accommodating, compromising, and collaborating—each of which can be effective depending on the situation. Other common tools include the Myers-Briggs Type Indicator (MBTI), which categorizes individuals into 16 personality types; the Enneagram, which identifies core motivations, fears, and desires across nine personality types; and questionnaires that assess physiological responses to perceived threats, such as fight, flight, freeze, or fawn reactions.

Awareness of your personality type, along with the impact of your communication and interactions, allows you to assist parties in understanding how their patterns may escalate conflict. When parties better understand themselves in relation to each other, this insight can shift how they interpret, value, and decide—often sparking changes in their behaviour. Noticing when behavioural changes lead to more productive outcomes strengthens both your personal growth and your effectiveness as a professional conflict intervenor. This is especially important when conflict behaviours escalate strong emotions or trigger defensive responses, such as arguing, attacking, resisting, blaming others, repeating a position, denying responsibility, or making excuses.

The questions below are designed to help you think about your conflict style. Reflect on a recent conflict at home, work, or in your community, and remember that your style may shift depending on your relationship with the other person and your role. Be sure to note your answers and insights in your Learning Journal.

> *How do you normally react when conflict first emerges? Do you avoid it? Become competitive and assertive? Do you accommodate by trying to please the angry person? Do you compromise by splitting the difference? Or do you welcome the opportunity to collaborate by taking the time to talk together?*
>
> *What learned 'rules' do you have for how you should behave in conflict? Who did you learn this from?*
>
> *What does being in conflict say about you? (For example, that you are not a good person, or that conflict is simply a normal part of life.)*
>
> *What conflict style do you strive to use more often?*
>
> *What behaviour in others prevents you from being curious about how they feel or think?*

Reflecting on how your upbringing, education, age, values, culture, and other social factors shape your worldview can help you understand your reactions and behaviour in conflict. Similarly, questions that surface others' values and worldviews can help you better understand what really matters to them. In addition to eliciting information, it is essential to confirm your interpretation is accurate. This is achieved through verifying questions such as:

> *Do I have it right that you thought I was intentionally trying to undermine your chances of a promotion?*
>
> *Am I correct in assuming you want to do this without any help from me?*
>
> *As I understand it you are nervous that you will not know anyone at the party?*

As you work through these activities, approach the questions with a spirit of self-knowledge and critical thinking. Deepening your understanding of yourself clarifies what matters most to you in conflict and fosters curiosity about others—an essential quality for helping people identify barriers to listening, learning, and understanding through constructive dialogue. Sustaining this curiosity, for both yourself and others, lies at the heart of becoming a self-reflective Insight practitioner.

Activities and Recommended Readings for Chapter Four

Use your *Learning Journal* to record your answers for each of the three activities below.

Activity 1

The focus in this activity is heightening awareness about patterns of communication and behaviours in conflict situations. To do this, think about a previous conflict, the emotions it surfaced, and how it was resolved.

> *How much of what you felt, and consequently did, in this situation is reminiscent of what you may have done in your youth at home and that now operates below the surface in the present?*
>
> *How is this way of responding keeping you locked in old patterns that are less useful now?*

Activity 2

For this exercise, I borrow from a conflict between a mother (Claudette) and her teenage daughter (Lauren) who disagree strongly over curfew times found on pages 132-146 in PIM. After you decide which role you are taking (either the MOTHER or the DAUGHTER) answer the following questions to gain insight into the patterns fueling this conflict.

> *What do your behaviours (as Claudette OR as Lauren) and your communication style, tell you about how much you care about 'what is at stake'? Consider how threatening the situation is for you as Claudette or Lauren? How are you defending, for example—Are you persuading? Repeating your point of view? Are you interrupting? Are you silent or refusing to listen? Are you willing to listen? Are you hopeful talking will make things better?*
>
> *What are you noticing (as Claudette OR as Lauren) about your conflict style, your assumptions and your feelings? For example: Are you angry? Are you shocked? Are you fearful? Are you feeling threatened? Are you tearful? Are you insistent about being 'right'?*
>
> *As you reflect on your style of responding in this conflict, ask yourself how effective or ineffective that response has been.*
>
> *Given what you are learning about Insight Mediation theory and practice, how can the ideas that: 1) conflict is a response to apprehensions of threat and 2) feelings are carriers of value help you change how you might respond to conflict in the future?*

Activity 3

This activity focuses on the 'Is It So' verifying question. Complete the questions in Appendix B (also the *'Insight Mediator Self-Assessment Tool,'* PIM Appendix E (pp. 177–179). As you reflect, use the 'Is It So' question to confirm your perceived progress accurately reflects your development as an Insight mediator. Broaden your verification by seeking feedback from peers, instructors, significant others, or participants in role-play sessions. This process invites reflection on the hallmarks of Insight Mediation in the present and serves as a tool for ongoing self-assessment and professional growth.

Recommended Reading

Re-read *'An Essay on Learning, Unlearning and Re-Learning'* in Appendix C. Reflect upon, then note your answers to, the questions below in your *Learning Journal*. Tracking these questions and the responses you provide may help create a deeper understanding of self-reflection, learning and growth.

> *How do you approach a new learning environment? For example, are you excited, are you worried? Are you able to think of how to integrate new ideas? Are you aware of your patterns (communication, conflict) especially the ones you do out of habit? How do you feel about this?*
>
> *Given that Insight Mediation is described as a 'process of discovery and learning', how can you use your interest and curiosity to open yourself to this new way of working with conflict?*
>
> *What is it about learning, and trying a new way of mediating that is threatening for you?*
>
> *The Insight approach calls on mediators to pay attention to noticing parties' self-focused dialogue, along with their feelings, personal and relational values. How does paying attention to this type of disclosure help a mediator learn? What kind of 'story' are you being told? What, if any concerns do you foresee with your ability to focus your attention on threat-to-care stories?*
>
> *What do you think is behind any difficulty you currently have with letting go of what you now know, and do, as a conflict practitioner?*
>
> *How committed are you to learning more about the Insight approach? If this is important to you, how will you continue this pursuit?*

NOTES

Insight's Alchemy

When we get mad and voices fly,
It's hard to see the reason why.

A threat to care can start the fight –
"You don't respect me!" "That's not right!"

Then comes the defend-attack parade,
A pattern of words that both have made.

But if we pause, and listen to see,
And ask with curiosity –

"What matters most? What's going on?"
The stormy feelings start to calm.

A learning conversation grows,
And insight helps the caring show.

New ways of seeing start to bloom,
As understanding fills the room.

L. Taylor 2025

APPENDICES

Journalling my Learning Experience and Insights
'Curiosity is the wick in the candle of learning (William Arthur Ward)

The following thoughts are in support of your learning journey and as you begin to incorporate what you learn about Insight Mediation into real-life situations.

First, LEARNING IS A JOURNEY. Be kind to yourself if, or when, the journey produces feelings of insecurity, frustration about not knowing, or feelings of threat if you do not get it all at once. Talk about these experiences with your colleagues, instructors, or significant others. Pay attention to, and reflect on, what you are noticing as you begin to link the ideas and skills to real-life situations. Record your thoughts, feelings and questions in a learning journal, which we are encouraging you to undertake as part of learning about Insight Mediation.

Second, be proud that you have taken steps to expand what you already know. Go at your own pace. Give yourself permission to be less of an expert as you work to un-learn in order to re-learn.

Third, throughout this Guide there are examples that illustrate the theory and practices that shape the role and purpose of an Insight mediator. Pages numbers that refer you to the book *Practising Insight Mediation* are also included for easy reference to important concepts and skills. Learners are encouraged to practice Insight skills and strategies by taking advantage of opportunities to practice alongside other learners, and to continually engage in reflective practice on your own and with your peers. Practice and self-reflection help you build upon prior knowledge and experiences as you learn to become a skilled Insight practitioner. What follows are suggestions for keeping a *Personal Learning Journal.*

What is a 'Learning Journal' and Why Keep One?

A *Learning Journal* is a way of systematically recording your thoughts, impressions, concerns, questions and reflections. It provides an informal yet focused opportunity to express whatever comes to mind as you read conflict and mediation materials, participate in practice sessions, attend training workshops, and engage in conversations with colleagues and significant others.

Kept with frequent and regular entries over months or years, *a Learning Journal* provides a growing picture of your understanding of conflict resolution and mediation theory and practice, your professional aspirations, and the ways in which your learning is unfolding. For some, it can be a tool for analyzing and solving both personal and professional problems; for others it is a source of new ideas and questions to be explored.

Keeping track of concerns and questions allows you to come back to them later so you can address them with new insights and perspectives. Your *Learning Journal* is a tool for thinking about, evaluating and bringing together your learning.

As you engage in learning about learning chronicling your thoughts and emotions during the process can be a powerful tool to help you unblock what is blocking your own ability to learn; in turn that knowledge and experience can be used when you are working to help your clients open their minds to learning in a mediation.

Setting personal learning goals for learning about Insight Mediation makes good sense. With this in mind, below are some possible learning goals and learning principles to help you get started formulating your own aspirations for engaging with the material in this Guide, and with those joining you on this journey.

What are Some Learning Goals that I May Want to Consider?

- Learning to notice and understand the patterns of interaction fueling conflict situations from the perspective of Insight theory.

- Learning new ways to engage with conflicting parties, and to be self-reflective with myself, in order to change conflict situations for the better.

- Reflecting on my own conflict intervention patterns through reflective practice and self-appropriation.

What are Some Learning Principles that Would be Helpful?

- Wonder, notice, imagine, engage, ask, while recognizing that all questions are good questions.

- Seeking to achieve understanding, while recognizing that understanding does not mean agreement.

- Listening first to understand before you speak to be understood, and staying curious and open-minded while being responsible with 'air time'.

- Suffering is optional—take care of yourself during your learning journey.

In What Ways Can a Learning Journal Be Helpful to Me?

- A Learning Journal is a way to ruminate upon your learning experiences and heighten your noticing.

- It can help you identify your strengths and weaknesses along with your personal preferences, values, biases, and emotional reactions to various learning activities.

- It can provide a way to evaluate your learning and development and help facilitate the integration of theory and practice.

- A Learning Journal is an excellent way to become a reflective practitioner. A reflective practitioner is someone who actively analyzes and learns from their own practice, regularly reflecting on their experiences, actions, and decisions to identify areas for improvement and enhance their professional performance.

How Can I Start and Continue to Write in my Learning Journal?

- Use a notebook specifically for this purpose.

- Each entry should include the date, a brief description of the situation or learning event, a reflective comment about your learning, assumptions, insights, feelings, questions, and, when possible, follow-up action, resources, or other 'to do' information.

- A Learning Journal is personal and will reflect your personality. Be creative. Be honest. Be thorough. Challenge yourself.

- Organize and write your observations, questions and comments without concern for just the right word and whether your spelling and grammar are correct; bullet form works well here, as do pictures, doodles and other visuals that express thoughts and emotions.

- It is useful to begin your Learning Journal with some self-reflective questioning. Here are a few thoughts to get you started:

  - Reflect on, and then make entries about, your reaction to particular ideas, questions, or comments from others.

- Recount an Insight analysis of a conflict in your personal or professional life by reflecting on what worked for you and what didn't.

- Record insights related to your values, bias, personal preferences, and conflict style.

- Jot down thoughts and questions about what you have been hearing and reading.

- Take note of media accounts of current conflicts paying attention to how they are being responded to. What patterns are you noticing? What defend patterns can you observe?

- No doubt you will find value in returning to your entries as your learning progresses.

Appendix B

Insight Mediator Self-Assessment Tool (PIM 177-179)

1. **Understanding the Process of Insight Mediation and the Dynamics of Conflict**

   ☐ What do I understand as the process and goal of Insight Mediation and my role in it?

   ☐ How well do I understand the concepts of learning, generating insights, meaning making, and interpretation?

   ☐ How would I define conflict to others?

   ☐ How able am I to convene a mediation session?

   ☐ How able am I to determine if a conflict situation is suitable for mediation?

2. **Ability to Provide an Effective Insight Mediation Process**

   ☐ How competent am I in each phase of the Insight Mediation process? Which phase is the most difficult and why?

   ☐ How do I plan to improve my abilities while working in this phase?

   ☐ How able am I to notice and help parties change their 'defend' patterns of interaction?

   ☐ How able am I to encourage perspective taking between the parties?

   ☐ How able am I to stimulate a creative exploration of new ways of interacting that would reduce threats?

   ☐ How able am I to help the parties explore and evaluate the consequences of these new interactions?

   ☐ How able am I to summarize what the parties agreed to, either in writing or in some other form?

3. **Analytical and Responsive Intentionality Skills**

   ☐ How able am I to understand the conflict situation and verify areas of threat?

   ☐ How able am I to think and act 'with responsive intentionality'?

   ☐ How able am I to help the parties discover their threats-to-cares and at what level the cares are operating?

   ☐ How able am I to discover the meaning-making that led to the parties' actions?

   ☐ How able am I to help the parties broaden their knowledge and understanding and surface the threats and defend responses that are contributing to the conflict?

   ☐ How able am I to help the parties deepen the learning conversation?

- ☐ How able am I to screen, retain, process, and synthesize information accurately and in the moment?
- ☐ How able am I to link the present with past experiences and expectations of an unwelcome or dire future?

4. Communication and Empathic Skills

- ☐ How able am I to speak in a clear, direct, confident and caring manner?
- ☐ How able am I to use the skills of listening to understand?
- ☐ How able am I to notice defend stories and avoid paraphrasing them?
- ☐ How able am I to ask curious and elicitive questions that uncover threats-to-cares and generate new insights?
- ☐ How able am I to verify that these insights are correct?
- ☐ How able am I to use deepening skills such as bridging, layering, finishing, and using?
- ☐ How comfortable am I with high emotion and using the skill of immediacy?
- ☐ How able am I to reflect emotions and deepen to discover what these feelings are about?
- ☐ How well do I understand the concept of feelings as carriers of values?
- ☐ How able am I to foster a relationship that is safe for the parties to express their emotions?

5. Overall Presence and Style as a Mediator

- ☐ How would I describe my personal style?
- ☐ How able am I to act with integrity, flexibility, and creativity?
- ☐ How able am I to be impartial and to demonstrate it to the parties?
- ☐ How able am I to provide a safe atmosphere in which to discuss threats-to-cares and defend responses?
- ☐ How able am I to instill confidence in mediation as a learning process?
- ☐ How confident am I to present myself in a way that demonstrates my ability as a mediator?
- ☐ Do I see myself working as a professional mediator in the future? If so, what do I see as my current limitations to working as a professional mediator?

An Essay on Learning, Unlearning and Re-Learning

Cheryl Picard, 2022

Learning to unlearn is the highest form of learning (Buddhist proverb)

INTRODUCTION

This essay emanates from noticing how challenging it can be for seasoned mediation practitioners as they begin to learn about, and then attempt to use, Insight Mediation theory and its associated skills. Part of this challenge may lie in the assumption that 'if I attend a workshop, or if I read the book Practising Insight Mediation, or if I listen to an Insight expert, I will be able to do what is being taught given that I am already an accomplished mediator.' Unfortunately, it is not that simple. Integrating ideas with the aim of changing long-standing patterns of conflict intervention is a complex and involved process that encompasses not just learning, but also unlearning and re-learning. It is my hope that this essay will shed light on the complexity of learning to re-learn, and in turn, lead to valuing the discomfort that may accompany your journey towards learning about the Insight approach to conflict and mediation.

LEARNING

'The mind needs to be well-stocked more with questions than with answers, else it will be closed and unable to learn' (Bernard Lonergan).

Changing unconscious and habitual ways of interacting with others to do something that is different and not yet fully understood, engages us in a series of mental operations. Picard and Melchin and Picard draw from the work of Bernard Lonergan to point out that learning is neither passive nor linear. It involves us in an ongoing and circular process comprises four distinct operations: 1) *Noticing and Experiencing*, 2) *Understanding and Insight*, 3) *Judging and Verifying,* and 4) *Valuing and Deciding*. Insight practitioners use these operations of learning, or operations of consciousness, to ask questions that will expand what parties know; help them make sense of conflict behaviours that make little or no sense; verify that new understandings are correct; imagine possible ways forward; and, then make decisions about how they will act moving forward. Mediation itself is a process of discovery and learning.

OPERATIONS OF LEARNING

Before discussing the phenomena of learning, unlearning and re-learning, it is useful to point out the links between operations of learning and the practice of Insight Mediation. To be transparent, my goal is to pique the reader's interest in a way that leaves them curious about the Insight approach and the excitement it is generating. It is from this place of curiosity that I hope learners will become interested in letting go, or at least try to, of their current ways of intervening in conflict and be motivated to put the time and effort into learning some new ways. Being able to do this requires that we first take the time to discover our habitual ways of interacting and then practice the new skills in order to build some 'muscle memory'. Experience tells me this can be scary. Thus, my invitation is to envisage what is being talked about in this paper, not as something radically new, but as something that builds on what you already know and do. A colleague of mine describes what I am saying in this way, 'mediators need to be invited into the possibility of a new order, an invitation that is radically new, but yet not; given that the learning is entangled'.

INSIGHT MEDIATION AND THE OPERATIONS OF LEARNING

Insight mediators focus their interventions toward expanding what parties know about themselves in relation to each other. At the core of their interventions is helping parties gain insights that help them make decisions on dealing with their differences in productive and lasting ways. Operations of learning are central to all that insight mediators do, functioning as a kind of 'operating system' for their work. These operations underpin the conviction that 'change happens through learning'. Insight mediators use these operations, and their related questions, to expand what parties

know about each other helping them discover non-threatening alternate paths for future interactions.

In the first operation, *Noticing and Experiencing*, the mediator pays particular attention to noticing parties defend patterns of talking about the conflict situation, and their defensive responses and behaviours towards others. Defending behaviours include repetitive explanations and elaborations, as well as justifying, blaming, self-excusing, accounting for, rationalizing, talking-over, and other self-focused responses that support existing views and actions. When any of these responses are noticed, an Insight mediator will focus attention on discovering the party's personal and relational values, or 'cares', that lie beneath the behaviours rather than asking about the details of what they understand as the party's 'defend story'. Asking about what a party is defending inadvertently invites them to expand on the 'wrongness' of the other, or the 'rightness' of themselves. This, in turn, reinforces the need for the listening party to defend more. When this happens, curiosity about each other becomes non-existent. The aim of the Insight mediator then becomes to surface the 'threat-to-care story' through threat-based questions such as:

- *What is it that troubles you?*
- *What is threatening about this situation?*
- *If you cannot be there every weekend, what do you fear will happen?*
- *What is making you so worried?*

- *What are the dangers in that request?*
- *What dire outcomes are you imagining?*
- *What are you trying to protect the children from?*
- *You are clearly hesitant, what worries you about that suggestion?*

Deepening on the answers to these questions surfaces any misunderstandings or incorrect interpretations about the other party's intentions. The Insight mediator's questions disrupt the certainty of parties knowing each other only as a threat generating uncertainty and curiosity about the other's intent and actions that expands knowing and generates new insights.

The second operation of learning, *Understanding and Insight*,' is where Insight mediators invite parties to enlarge their 'mental maps' through conversations that generate deeper understanding through new insights. Of course, changing a party's mental map is not easy. For one thing, they have deeply embedded knowledge and core values learned from their families, schools, the media, organized religion, governments, and so forth. Each of these present reality through a specific lens: realities commonly followed unconsciously. The more people learn about a particular reality, be it true or false, the more rigid their views become and the less able they are to imagine other possibilities, or act in other ways. In this operation, we notice the Insight mediator asking about interpretations, assumptions and meaning-making.

- *What are you hearing her say to you?*
- *When he does not reply to your text, what is he telling you?*
- *When you sent that letter, what did you expect her to do?*
- *How do you interpret the fact that nothing has changed?*
- *How does it feel when you are asked questions about your family back home?*
- *When she acts out, how do you feel?*
- *When you feel that way, what do you do?*
- *How do you make sense of the fact that your problem with him keeps re-surfacing?*

Insight mediators also know to pay attention to what is going on within themselves, what they are learning, and how that learning is influencing their interventions and impacting their emotions. Paying attention to what is going on with ourselves in the moment is important: 'When mediators have learned the skills of understanding their own operations of questioning and insight, they can identify more accurately these operations in others. They can help parties gain self-understanding and can help them become curious about the cares and concerns of others (Melchin & Picard, 2008).' Self-reflection is a concept long advanced in the field of conflict resolution and mediation. A key leader in this area is Michael Lang (2019).

Judging and Verifying is the third operation of learning. It is in this stage that Insight mediators focus less on producing expanded knowing and more on verifying that the expanded understandings and new insights are correctly understood by the parties and by themselves. Verifying is a critical com-ponent of learning; for while parties may have insights, they can be wrong! Successful decision-making on alternate paths forward necessitates that new understandings are accurate. Questions asked by the mediator might include:

- *My understanding of what you are saying is…, Do I have that right?*
- *It seems the most important aspect now is settling the visitation schedule; is this correct?*
- *Based on what she just said, does she understand you?*
- *Let me confirm what I think you are saying.*

The mediator will more often ask parties what they are hearing the other say as a way to verify their interpretations and meaning-making are correct. For instance,

- *What are you hearing her say about the need for flexibility?*
- *What meaning are you attaching to his unwillingness to entertain your request?*
- *When she talks about how hard life is, what is she telling you?*
- *The fact that he is often late picking up the children says what to you?*

Questions are mediators' most powerful learning tool. They invite parties to get involved personally in new ways of thinking and feeling, and they: 'help direct the parties' attention to things they may have escaped notice. But because the mediator offers these possibilities to disputants as questions

rather than as statements, power over the process remans in the hands of the parties themselves. It is they who have to hit on the insights, and insights can never be managed (Picard, 2003).'

Valuing and Deciding is the fourth operation of learning. For Insight mediators this means helping parties make decisions about how to act upon what they now know through curious questions directed at discovering how much what they now know matters; what they think they should do about it; and, what they will do about it. Exploring parties 'valuing' of their expanded knowing helps them discover alternate paths for collaborative decision-making.

- *It seems you are ready to explore ways of interacting that will not trigger defensive reactions in each other. What are some of the ideas that come to mind?*
- *It is likely that some of the ideas you feel strongly about; which ones are at the top of the list and which ones can you live without if you had to?*
- *Which ideas do you feel the most confident in following through on?*
- *Which ideas are you less sure you can agree to?*

It is common for parties to expect others will change simply because they understand more about each other's needs. Under-standing, however, does not necessarily mean agreement. Talking about how much a particular viewpoint or request matters is critical when parties are searching for alternate and less threatening paths forward.

UNLEARNING

'The first problem for all of us, men and women, is not to learn, but to unlearn' (Gloria Steinem).

The Cambridge Dictionary defines unlearning as 'making an effort to forget your usual way of doing something so that you can learn a new and sometimes better way.' For many of us, and certainly for parties in conflict being asked to listen to those they disagree with can be quite unsettling because it means getting out of our comfort zone. It forces us to let go of our past assumptions and beliefs which have likely been with us much of our life. Questioning can sometimes feel like questioning our whole being. It may feel like a personal attack; worse still: a personal attack done by us to ourselves. For sure this is the case when we focus on what we have to lose by letting go of old knowledge rather than thinking about what we might stand to gain. When we are questioning, but our friends or colleagues are not, we may find ourselves shying away from the group because we see our work from a new perspective while they carry on with their existing ways leaving us less certain about what they are thinking of us. They may even feel threatened by our new views. Nevertheless, when we have those 'aha moments' that start us asking the right questions we know the only way is forward, there is no going back.

The first step to unlearning is to be open to it by looking forward to a new and better tomorrow. Insight mediators, right from the get-go, ask parties about their 'hopes for a better future if they are successful today in engaging in dialogue about ways to improve the situation for themselves and for each other'. While being open and hopeful may sound obvious, it is not so easy given that much of our knowledge is deeply rooted within ourselves and manifests through automatic behaviour. Breaking old patterns requires identifying the old knowledge before assimilating new knowledge. It means letting go of previous ideas by cultivating an almost 'blank page' approach to the situation; as in a child with insatiable curiosity. The second step is to chase the unfamiliar. Putting yourself regularly into new situations allows you to see the world from a new perspective. Ditch the comfort, put yourself out there and watch it happen. Become excited and hopeful about the new you, you are creating. As a conflict professional learning new ideas and skills, Albert Einstein's quote is reassuring: 'we cannot solve our problems with the same thinking we used when we created them'.

Below are some relevant questions to reflect on at each level of your learning journey.

1) Experiencing and Noticing: *What am I noticing about me in this learning situation? What am a noticing about others? How does what I am noticing make me feel?*

2) Understanding and Insight: *What am I really being taught? How has what I am learning changed what I knew before? How will this impact me going forward?*

3) Judging and Verifying: *Do I fully understand what I am learning? How can*

I confirm that I understand what is being taught?

4) Valuing and Deciding: *How important is it to me that I learn this well? What should I be doing now that I have learned this? Will I actually do what needs to be done?*

The sooner we set our minds to the need to 'unlearn', the sooner we can get at it. That said, the mind can be 'slow to unlearn what it learned early', and some people find themselves set in their ways to the point of feeling bound by the beliefs they once held. Once those grooves are made in the brain and reinforced over time, it takes something extraordinary to reprogram over them. Furthermore, when what we believe to be true gets reinforced by other people, who believe the same thing, it becomes more deeply validated in our minds. Bruce Lipton (2008) studies how subconscious 'habitual' perceptions work in the now through our cells. Helpful to us is the discovery that some of the most powerful external signals that influence the health of our cells are the energetic messages which emanate from our thoughts. This is great news because it means that 'limiting beliefs' can be changed, and that we have the power to alter our lives for the better! We can control our destiny.

Unlearning and then re-learning is meant to touch all areas of our lives - from the personal to the professional to the social. Questioning at the personal level may include asking ourselves why we want to work with people in conflict? What is driving us to be better at it? What do we fear about changing what we currently do? At the professional level we may wonder about how we came to follow our current conflict intervention and mediation practices? Who told us to do what we do, and how do we know if we are doing it? If we change, how will our colleagues view us? At the social level our curiosity may be directed at how to more effectively work with large conflicted and combatant groups of people. We may even wonder if the work we are doing will ever bring peace to those encumbered in civil conflicts? Then again, we may wonder if the changes we pursue will be realized in our lifetime.

Creating the possibility for change is about acknowledging that just because something is a certain way, it doesn't have to remain that way. In our rapidly changing world, unlearning and relearning are as critical as continuous, acquisitive learning. Yet in our 'always on' lives it can be challenging to know what to learn, and then find the time to do it. Unlearning is about knowing what to give up. It requires self-analysis and having the confidence to discard what is no longer true, relevant, or helpful.

In my Insight Mediation trainings, I engage participants in various self-reflective activities, encouraging them not to dwell too much on the questions, given that there are no right or wrong answers; this exercise is about learning more about you. For instance, I ask about the worldviews they hold about why people behave as they do (i.e., people are born good; we can control our destiny; power is fixed; people can change). I also ask them to think about their beliefs relating to conflict behaviour (i.e., people are always trying to get more than their fair share; conflict is bad; the best way to deal with conflict is to fix it so it does not happen again; we should avoid talking about emotions and values in conflict). And, I ask what, if any, of their beliefs may be holding them back from achieving satisfactory outcomes in their own conflicts (if I listen, it will appear as if I agree; if I give-in, I loose; it is best to hide how I feel). After participants learn more about Insight theory and practice, I then ask them to reflect on their personal conflict behaviours and mediation interventions that, from experience, they might want to unlearn and then re-learn. If they choose to adjust their practice more toward the Insight method, I refer them to my 'Insight Mediator Self-Assessment Tool' (*Practicing Insight Mediation* 2016:177) to help them self-reflect on their competency.

Self-reflective tools can also be helpful when striving to change 'knee-jerk' conflict behaviours. Conflict imagery is one such example. Imagine this: you are in a heated debate where angry words are flying like arrows to a target. Imagine calming yourself by counting slowly one... two... three... four... five... then repeat and wait for your defensive negative energy to lessen. Picture yourself moving a target from over your heart, where words feel hurtful and lead to anger, to moving the target to your side where the arrows cannot touch you. Imagine you have a giant bubble around you keeping you safe from the arrows and angry words landing beside you. Imagine your feet are rooted to the ground and that you are drawing strength from it to stay balanced and focused enabling you to calmly respond instead of knee-jerk react. Being calm and collected helps us decide what we want to do and say. Make an effort to listen first and respond second. Breathe... Breathe some more... Verify that you understand what is being said. Share your thoughts in non-blaming and non-accusatory language.

Visualizing goals and exercising mind-fulness are other tools to assist with learning, unlearning and relearning. In fact, there is an abundance of self-help techniques designed to help you identify old knowledge that no longer serves you, and that can help you let go of limiting beliefs in order to assimilate new ones. Many these self-help books provide experiential activities designed to access the personal and advance personal growth. I encourage you to seek those most suited to your own learning journey. One suggestion to get you started is Eugene Gendlin's (1978, 1981) work on felt-sense, focusing and decision-making.

It is clear after many years of teaching, that attempting to 'unlearn' the knowing that contributes to our sense of identity and self-worth is tough. I constantly notice this with seasoned and respected mediators who come to Insight training workshops. For them, it is a real challenge to engage in learning that contradicts what they already know and that leaves them feeling uncertain, less competent, and less of an expert in their own right. Yet their determination to learn something that they believe will make them better at what they do is often strong enough for them to hang in and work through the discomfort that comes with their learning.

When I notice frustration and anxiety in learners, I draw from Broadwell's work on the Levels of Learning to talk about how learning to do something different happens in stages and takes time. Learning about learning is a comfort because it normalizes their own experiences, and they can see themselves in the various levels. When teaching Insight Mediation skills, I talk about Broadwell's levels this way:

Level One

Unaware and Unable: you are unaware of Insight Mediation and feel anxious about learning in front of strangers or peers. You are unsure how relevant it will be for you, and you are anxious about being able to do what is being taught.

Level Two

Aware and Unable: you begin to see the value of new ideas and want to learn. You feel frustrated by your inability to easily use the skills, yet you are motivated to continue practicing. You under-stand the concepts but still can't act on them quite yet. You seek help from the instructor and other learners; you really want to learn.

Level Three

Aware and Able: you become excited as you begin to experience the usefulness of this method. You want to be good at doing it and become determined to get over the last few hurdles. You recognize the times when your skills work, while at other times, you still feel awkward and

you need to pause and think before progressing.

Level Four

Unaware and Able: you are able to use the skills without always thinking first. Your experience is such that the skills are almost second nature. You have reached mastery.

Level Five

Self-appropriation: you can critically reflect and self-assess your ability to correctly use the skills; your advanced knowledge enables you to teach the Insight method to others.

RE-LEARNING

'The illiterate of the 21st century will not be those who cannot read and write, but those who cannot learn, unlearn, and relearn' (Alvin Toffler).

Recent insights into neuroplasticity highlight the ability of our brain to both unlearn and re-learn by creating new and strengthened pathways through the neurons of the brain; it is the scientific basis for the growth mindset. Those working in the field of neuroplasticity believe we can choose to either have a fixed mindset, or a growth mindset. They tell us that if we choose the latter, it will help us to embrace the opportunity for creating new and more productive habits and behaviours. And, that choosing a growth mindset is what allows us to take on new lifestyles, for instance, artful aging programs that inspire and enable adults to learn, make and share in ways that are novel, complex and socially engaging. Similarly, staying sharp activities and games designed to boost health, knowledge, self-awareness and work-life-balance create value for us. Neuroscience researchers talk about 'flow' as a means of stretching well beyond our capabilities in order to reach peak performance.

Insight practitioners can learn from neuroscientists; what they promote is not magic. It involves being open to change by having a willingness to accept the challenge, persevering through the challenge, and a desire to embrace a 'new you.' The following suggestions may help you to embrace the learning, unlearning, relearning cycle of mediation advancement.

- Spend time reflecting on the idea of unlearning and relearning and setting challenges for yourself that focus on your knowledge, skills, identity, and habits. The Insight Mediation self-assessment tool in my book (2016) was designed with this purpose in mind.
- Request feedback from someone you trust to give yourself fresh perspectives on your personal conflict behaviour or on your professional conflict practice.
- Ensure that you are staying up-to-date with the knowledge and skills that are relevant to your profession and your success.
- Seek a mentor who will help to support and challenge you on your learning journey.

- Learning, unlearning and re-learning is a complex and ongoing process. The following illustration reminds us of the four operations of learning leading to new understanding generated from unlearning and relearning resulting in new behaviours that create new experiences (for ourselves and others). It reminds us that learning is continuous as it loops back to the operations of learning creating an on-going cycle.

CONCLUSION

People are social animals, and from a very young age we are continuously learning how to behave in groups. A study done in 2016 from Ludwig-Maximilians-Universität München, revealed that 'three-year-olds not only learn social norms from direct instruction, approval and disapproval, but they also seek norms themselves, even inferring them where adults see none.' This deriving what ought to be from what is, while essential for growth and the ability to interact with others, means we end up learning things that are not necessarily true or useful. Clinging to old, outdated knowledge hinders our ability to progress. Here is a Zen story that depicts this:

An emperor asks a Zen monk how he can improve in life. The monk listens politely to the story and the question of the emperor. Then he asks if the emperor wants a cup of tea. The monk pours the tea into the cup, even when it is already full. The emperor watches the scene, and at the end, he can't help intervening. He yells: 'What are you doing, you see that the cup has been full for a while and you continue pouring tea...' 'Exactly,' says the monk. 'And it is the same with you. You are already full with your own ideas and conceptions. And you ask me to add more? First empty your cup and then it will be possible to pour some more.'

Earlier I mentioned Steven Kotler and his flow triggers that release dopamine in the body and get us to a state of flow allowing us to achieve peak performance. These flow triggers could also help us create a re-learning attitude about our mediation practice. Such an attitude would involve us in a number of actions: taking risks, embracing novelty, dealing with complexity, facing unpredictability, noticing patterns in our behaviours, fostering curiosity, and questioning everything.

In 1943, the president of IBM, Thomas Watson, said that he thought, 'there is a world market for maybe five computers.' This is a classic example of thinking based on out-of-date knowledge and assumptions, and a great example of the need to learn, unlearn, relearn the assumptions we make and the knowledge we hold! As conflict professionals we need to be able to continuously learn, unlearn and relearn if we are to stay relevant in a changing workforce. Skills have a limited shelf-life. If we assume we have 'life-long' skills that don't need to be relearnt we're in serious danger of becoming irrelevant and outdated. Whether it's learning to use new technology in the age of Covid or learning to deal with conflict differently so we can be better at it, we need to continuously learn, unlearn, relearn skills.

The final point I want to make is that adult learning brings with it many of the effective and ineffective learning experiences we had as children. Where some of us experienced school as a safe, exciting and fun place to be, others experienced it as an intimidating, humiliating and threatening place to be. Those experiences from the past follow us into the present and can influence the joy, or the burden, of learning. Accessing our unconscious through self-reflection is paramount in coming to understand how we think, feel and behave. The activities of learning, unlearning and re-learning provide space in the 21st century for non-duality thinking that invites learners into a new dimension that holds potential for real change.

So, get yourself a journal. Capture your learning journey. The ups and the downs. The joys and the disappointments. Notice how your life is changing, how the new Insight concepts and skills you are learning hold promise for improving both your personal and professional engagement in conflict. Do this on a consistent basis, perhaps over the course of a month or two or more. I am confident you will begin to notice that you are growing and changing. And that you are experiencing the energy of excitement that is filling you with all that is now possible. Enjoy the new perspectives you will have! Enjoy your learning journey.

BIBLIOGRAPHY

Doidge, Norman, The Brain that Changes Itself, Viking Publishers, 2007.

Lang, Michael, The Guide to Reflective Practice in Conflict Resolution, Rowman and Littlefield, 2019.

Lipton, Bruce, The Biology of Belief, Mountain of Love, 2005.

Lonergan, Bernard, Collected Works of Bernard Lonergan, Vol 3, Insight: A Study of Human Understanding. Toronto: University of Toronto Press, 1992.

Melchin, Kenneth and Cheryl Picard. Transforming Conflict through Insight, Toronto: University of Toronto Press, 2008.

Picard, Cheryl A., Practising Insight Mediation, Toronto: University of Toronto Press, 2016.

Picard, Cheryl A., 'Learning about Learning - The Value of Insight,' Conflict Resolution Quarterly, Vol. 20, No. 4, pp. 477-484, 2003.

Price, Jamie, 'Method in Analyzing Conflict Behaviour: The Insight Approach,' Revista de Mediacion, Vol. 11, No 1, 2017.

Four Distinguishing Features of Insight Mediation

Cheryl Picard and Kenneth Melchin, 2022

Insight Mediation brings conflicting parties together in face-to-face dialogue sessions that help them transform conflicts by gaining insights into them-selves and others. Insight mediators help parties probe feelings of threat that block them from innovating solutions on their own. Through insights they de-link from threat feelings, and this opens avenues for a genuine curiosity that can explore more cooperative and less threatening ways of interacting. The process is fully participatory, creative, flexible, emergent, non-linear, and responsive. It takes parties through a five-phase process towards decisions that change their conflicts for the better.

At first glance, Insight Mediation may appear similar to other mediation models. With roots in Insight Theory, however, the training takes practitioners in novel directions that are markedly different, and for this reason it is currently acclaimed as a fourth pillar of mediation. We believe that exploring its full potential has only just begun. There are four features that distinguish Insight Mediation from other approaches:

1. Conflict is understood as arising from threats-to-cares;

2. Conflicts evoke feelings and narratives that block parties from innovating solutions on their own;

3. Conflict is resolved through the transformative learning of insights; and

4. Insight mediators help parties by deepening on threats-to-cares.

CONFLICT IS UNDERSTOOD AS ARISING FROM THREATS-TO-CARES

In Insight Mediation, conflict is understood differently than in other mediation approaches. Instead of thinking of conflict as arising from incompatible or conflicting goals, needs, or interests, conflict is said to emerge from defending behaviours animated by feelings of threat to an individual's or group's 'cares'; an occurrence referred to as 'threats-to-cares.'

Cares are understood to be of various types and they operate on various levels. What is important for Insight mediators is the distinction between two levels of cares: (1) cares for particular goods that satisfy our own particular interests, needs and desires, and (2) cares rooted in deeper patterns of interpersonal or social cooperation that evoke strong value feelings, which oblige us, often without our being aware, toward actions focused on others. While parties usually can identify their cares of the first type, frequently they have not understood their own deeper cares of the second type. The deeper cares drive conflict behaviours through feelings, images, and narratives that often operate pre-reflectively. When these cares are threatened, even when parties have not under-stood their own deeper cares, they nonetheless feel the need to defend themselves or attack others.

As in other models, Insight mediators can help parties probe beyond presenting problems to identify underlying cares of the first type. But this is not their main task. Rather, their focus is on probing the deeper threats that operate as blocks to understanding. This means that Insight mediators must help parties gain insights into themselves as well as each other.

In conflict situations, it is easy for parties to misunderstand each other's words and actions, and these misunderstandings arise frequently when threat feelings shift them towards defending and away from curiosity and understanding. Under-standing others requires that we be curious about them, that we be open to alternate lines of questioning, that we consider things from their perspective, that we learn about their context, that we gain the necessary insights, and that we ask the questions required for verifying our insights and correcting our misunderstandings. When we feel threatened, our minds are galvanized into action away from these concerns and towards defending matters to us. The result is our minds get blocked and we are left with the misunderstandings that exacerbate conflicts.

The main task of Insight mediators is to probe these threats-to-cares so they can help parties de-link from the blockages that escalate and sustain conflicts. When they do

this successfully, parties are able to innovate solutions for themselves.

CONFLICTS EVOKE FEELINGS AND NARRATIVES THAT BLOCK PARTIES FROM INNOVATING SOLUTIONS ON THEIR OWN

The Insight approach recognizes that parties in conflict interpret the meanings and actions of others based on data from two different sources: (1) data from their careful observations of others; and (2) data from feelings and narratives from their own past that are triggered in the present by the words and actions of others. When parties' responses are animated by threats-to-cares, then data from the second source (their own feelings and narratives) often distort their interpretations of others and block the curiosity required for correcting these distortions. When Insight mediators probe parties' threats-to-cares, their goal is to discover the personal feelings and narratives that influence these misunderstandings so they can be discovered and more accurately understood.

Conflicts are patterns of interaction happening in the present that are linked to experiences of the past that give rise to expectations of unwelcome futures. To exemplify this point, we refer to the workplace mediation between Les and Micki analyzed in Dr Picard's book (Chapter 4), *Practising Insight Mediation*. In this dispute it was discovered that how Micki and her co-workers responded to a request by Les to answer the phones over their lunch-hour triggered in him feelings of threat, and that these feelings were accompanied by an unformulated yet powerful narrative that was rooted in Les' past. The narrative provided Les with a 'logic' for his defending behaviour that the staff interpreted as an attack on them—a logic that in their minds felt perfectly reasonable and justified. In Les' past experience, when others spoke and acted like this, the result was that harm came to him. The narrative placed Les in the present with the expectation that an unwelcome event in the future will happen, and so he must now focus entirely on defending against this. The same sort of threat-based experience is also taking place for Micki and the co-workers she represents.

In Insight Mediation, we expect to discover that conflicting parties' interpretations of each other are likely mistaken. These misunderstandings arise because when a party feels threatened, the feelings and narratives triggered from their own past (data from the second source) block the curiosity required for carefully attending to the words and actions of others (data from the first source). The work of the Insight mediator, then, is to ask questions that elicit answers that can help correct these misunderstandings. One strategy is for the mediator to ask Les for his interpretation of the staff's actions, and then to ask Micki to verify if that is what they were intending. Because the questions were careful enough to elicit the personal feelings and narratives that shaped Les' interpretations, Micki was able to discover information that helped her correct important misunderstandings.

When Insight mediators ask parties questions that probe for unwelcome futures, they often unearth responses that have the greatest potential for transforming conflicts. When the mediator asked Les about his expectations of a dire future, her focus was as much on Micki as it was on Les. The mediator was interested in observing and learning how Micki was listening and responding to the conversation going on with Les. In particular, she was interested in Micki's reaction to the portrait of the conflict that was emerging. Breakthroughs occurred when Les formulated an account of a dire future expectation that was sufficiently different from the actual intentions of Micki and the other staff causing Micki to sit up and take notice. She became curious in a way that previously she was not. This curiosity helped her de-link from her prior portrait of the conflict with its implied threat to her and the other staff's deeper cares.

CONFLICT IS RESOLVED THROUGH THE TRANS-FORMATIVE LEARNING OF INSIGHTS

A key aspect that differentiates Insight Mediation from other approaches is that it engages parties in a learning process to resolve conflict. Learning, when it is authentic, is transformative, and this changes the course of conflicts. The mediator's focus is on opening pathways for the curiosity that sets parties on the road to the transformative learning of insight.

Insight mediators do not help parties solve problems. Rather, they focus on helping remove blockages that stand in the way of parties solving problems for themselves. Frequently this involves learning that the problem is different from what they had thought. This means that Insight mediators pay attention to the kind and quality of learning of conflicting parties. They wonder about how curious parties are about each other and how able they are to be attentive to new information. When opportunities arise to probe threats that block curiosity, mediators ask questions that deepen parties' understanding of threats-to-cares.

Insight Mediation does not understand learning as acquiring information. Rather, the focus is not on acquiring information but on understanding information. This changes things dramatically. When we gain insights, we are transformed away from mistaken and misleading impressions and we begin to glimpse novel and surprising aspects of others that previously we would not have considered or imagined. When learning is blocked by threat feelings, parties' interpretations often misrepresent the other's intent leaving them feeling forced into defend behaviours. When parties are able to de-link from threat feelings, parties engage in ways they could not have done previously. Their new forms of engagement arise from initial insights that open the doors of curiosity. And what follows is a learning path animated by their basic 'operating system,' their curious mind's own operations of experiencing, understanding, verification, and decision. The goal of Insight mediators is to enhance the quality of

learning because of its potential for bringing about transformation and change.

INSIGHT MEDIATORS HELP PARTIES BY DEEPENING THE CONVERSATION ON THREATS-TO-CARES

The fourth distinguishing feature of Insight Mediation is that practitioners explore and deepen on the threats-to-cares at the root of the experience of attack and subsequent defend responses that generate and sustain conflict. For conflict to change, threat experiences need to be reduced or eradicated. Deepening the learning conversation helps parties determine whether their cares must necessarily threaten others' cares. It is the felt necessity of threat that keeps parties locked in conflict. If they can discover that differing cares can co-exist without the necessity of threat, the course of the conflict changes dramatically.

Misinterpretations in conflict result frequently in parties attributing intentions to others that are misguided. These attributions arise from the feelings and narratives from parties' own pasts that are triggered by the words and actions of others in the present. When their own narratives trigger parties into expectations of dire futures, the threats are attributed to others as their malicious intentions. In conflict, we generally feel like the other intends the harm we expect and fear. The fact remains, however, that these attributions are often enough misguided.

Deepening conversations help parties learn about their own feelings, narratives, and threats as well as those of the other party. Having threats 'on the table' allows them to be examined, considered, and reconsidered when they are found to be misguided. Paying attention to threats is the focus of deepening. Rather than helping parties innovate solutions, deepening focuses on the things parties frequently find difficult to talk about: their deeper cares, the feelings that accompany and evoke these cares, and the past life narratives that are triggered when these cares are threatened. These are the things holding them in conflict and when they can be discussed openly, insights transform the course of the conflict. At this point, parties are able to innovate solutions for themselves both today and in future conflicts.

There is much more to be said about deepening the learning conversation and the strategies mediators employ to deepen on threats-to-cares. For the present purposes, our focus is on offering a brief overview of four features that distinguish Insight Mediation from other approaches. Readers interested in reading further can consult the texts and bibliographies of two books we've published on Insight Mediation: Kenneth R. Melchin and Cheryl A. Picard, *Transforming Conflict through Insight* (Toronto: University of Toronto Press, 2008); and Cheryl A. Picard, *Practising Insight Mediation* (Toronto: University of Toronto Press, 2016). We also look forward to posting other texts on Insight Mediation on this website in the upcoming months. So please stay tuned

Appendix E

Setting a Strong Foundation for a Learning Conversation in Insight Mediation: The power of asking about hopes for an imagined better future

Cheryl Picard and Marnie Jull, 2023

INTRODUCTION

Mediators use a variety of communication skills in their work—such as paraphrasing, curious questioning and validating—to help conflicting parties address their differences and interact more peaceably. A mediator's choice of an intervention skill is based on their understanding of how conflict begins and changes. Asking about hopes for an imagined better future is a specific strategy used by mediators using the Insight approach because of their understanding of conflict that is quite different from other mediators. Their interventions are based on the understanding that conflict is enacted through people's behaviours. Conflict behaviour is what people do—when they discern some kind of threat and decide to defend—with behaviours like aggressive fighting, silence, avoidance or even placating appeasement. People enact those conflict behaviours when they believe they need to protect against different kinds of threat—including a risk to a practical interest or a concern about justice and fairness in systems. [1]

Other mediators, for example, may understand conflict to be the result of unmet needs so they would use questioning or paraphrasing skills to help the parties explore their needs as well as to consider ways to satisfy those needs in less conflictual ways. [2]

A different mediator might understand conflict to be an expression of competing narratives and power-related discourses, so the aim of the mediator's questioning or paraphrasing skills would be to help the parties to recognize and change those narratives in such a way as to alter the parties' interactions with each other.

What is distinct about Insight Mediation is the recognition of the truncating impact of threat on people's ability to listen and learn as well as the connection between a person's sense of threat and their defend-conflict behaviours. The impact of threat on cognitive functioning is to truncate curiosity and focus attention on defending and protecting in ways that are often habitual or rash. Insight Mediation is a way for parties to change their conflict behaviours. Using a range of strategies and communication skills, a mediator using the Insight approach helps parties expand their curiosity and counter the truncating impact of threat, which enable the parties to reassess their assumptions and interpretations shift their behaviours. An Insight-oriented mediator thus facilitates learning conversations by helping the parties become more curious and discover new possibilities in their interactions with the other. They do this through five overlapping and non-linear activities: 1) Attend to Process, 2) Broaden

Understanding, 3) Deepen Insights, 4) Explore Possibilities, and 5) Make Decisions. [3]

In this short essay we explore the theory and practice of the activities that take place before and in the early part of a mediation session to help a mediator and the parties create the foundation for a learning conversation. We begin with a brief introduction to 'Convening,' sometimes referred to as pre-mediation or intake, that happens before the joint sessions, along with an explanation of the activity that 'Attends to Process' [4]. The remainder of the paper will focus on 'Broadening Understanding,' with particular attention to the purpose and value of asking the parties about their imagined hopes for a better future, known in the Insight approach as the 'hope question.' To help us illustrate these activities we explore a simulated conflict named, 'What to do with Mom.'

The conflict revolves around two sisters —Adrianna and Carla—who disagree on how best to look after their mother, who is 87 years of age and living in the large home where she raised her family. Carla (who is divorced, has no children and a good job) lives in a small apartment. Adrianna (who does not work outside the home and is married with three children and two pets) lives in a large house. Although each sibling has concerns about their mother's ability to look after herself, they disagree about what to do. Adrianna thinks Carla should move in with their mother in the family home. Carla thinks her mom should move in with Adrianna. The sisters' arguments have reached a stage where they are no longer talking to each other, and neither one wants to upset their mother, who is not aware that these conversations are taking place. Their mother wants each daughter to be happy, does not want to be a bother to either one, and considers herself well enough to look after herself, despite a number of minor incidents that indicate she is having some challenges. Carla emailed Adrianna to suggest mediation. Adrianna agreed.

CONVENING A MEDIATION AND ATTENDING TO PROCESS

In separate sessions held prior to any joint sessions being held, the mediator talks with each sister in such a way as to set the stage for learning to take place during the mediation. In these one-on-one conversations, the mediator introduces herself and describes Insight Mediation as an opportunity for each sister to listen and be heard so that they can discover new possibilities for action. Through these convening conversations, the mediator also assesses whether the situation is appropriate for mediation and if the parties are sufficiently motivated to participate.

During the convening, pre-mediation or intake session, the mediator is attentive to helping the parties set the stage for learning from each other in the joint sessions that will follow. This involves strategically asking questions to prompt each sister to reflect on what matters to them as well as the certainties and patterns of interaction that prevent the two of them from agreeing or discovering their own solutions. Having this conversation with the mediator, without the other present, can help each sister engage her curiosity toward herself and possibly her sister in a way that may have not been accessible before.

The mediator also emphasises their role is as a facilitator rather than a decision-maker and discusses responsibilities for decision-making as well as confidentiality with each sister. The mediator also welcomes questions about the mediation process and asks each sister to consider what they might need in the session to feel comfortable and be able to listen or feel heard by the other. Once questions have been answered and there is agreement to proceed with joint sessions, a time, date and place will be set for the mediation.

The mediators' goal in the first joint session, because they recognize that a sense of threat inhibits the parties' capacity to listen and learn, is to help settle participants into the space and the conversation so they can be ready to engage. In our case study, the mediator takes some time to welcome Carla and Adrianna, and review their under-standings of roles, responsibilities and process that were discussed in convening. The parties are not the only ones to benefit from this opening phase: the mediator can also use this phase as a way to settle into listening and learning.

An Insight mediator 'attends to process' rather than 'introduces a process' for several reasons. Their role is to attend to process (i.e. the parties' interactions and the flow of dialogue) throughout the mediation, not just in the opening phase. 'Introducing a process' conveys an impression that the process belongs to the mediator, while 'attending to

process' is a task that can be shared by the parties and the mediator, who are co-responsible for how the mediation process evolves. An Insight mediator does not provide 'ground rules' but can help co-create guidelines with the parties. Being seen to establish rules can put the mediator in an authoritative role of referee rather than facilitator of a process that belongs with the parties. Instead, the mediator may say something like:

'Let's start by talking about what the two of you understand about mediation based on what we've talked about in our meetings. That way if there are questions or different understandings, we can talk about them to ensure we have a shared understanding of what will happen today. Next, we may want to talk about our roles - how I see my role and what you see as your role, along with what you need from each other, and from me, to make this a safe and successful dialogue. Remember, you are here to learn what really matters to each other and in the process, you are likely to discover more about what really matters to you. Learning how conflict behaviours are linked to protecting what you each value is often the door through which you will discover new ways of interacting with each other and making decisions that will be less painful and more productive.'

Using an elicitive and interactive learning process right from the start helps ensure the parties and the mediator agree on important aspects of the mediation such as roles, confidentiality, timelines, authority to make decisions and other process issues. [5] Furthermore, interacting with the parties in an inclusive manner enables the mediator to observe how willing, or capable, they are to engage with each other this early in the process. These observations of the parties' relative openness to listening and learning thus helps the mediator orient their strategies toward unblocking the flow of curiosity that can help the parties have a learning conversation.

After the sisters are settled into their process, the mediator asks each of them to talk about their hopes for a better tomorrow by choosing to attend mediation. This begins the second phase of Insight Mediation.

BROADENING UNDERSTANDING THROUGH THE HOPE QUESTION

Asking each party about their vision for a better tomorrow aims to reveal a different and less accusatory narrative from the one parties are used to hearing from each other. It intentionally avoids asking 'what is the problem you want to resolve' or 'what are the issues you have come to talk about.' Opening comments are seen as an opportunity for the parties to articulate their purpose and hopes in coming to mediation rather than to inadvertently regurgitate their disagreements, defend their viewpoints or reinforce their conflict behaviours. We will repeat this important point, considering that it may be a new idea for non-insight trained mediators. An Insight mediator does not invite the parties to make opening statements about the problem or issues to be discussed. These kinds of opening statements are often accusatory narratives

(what an Insight mediator might call 'defend stories'). [6] An Insight mediator understands these blame-filled stories are likely to elicit a sense of threat and reciprocal conflict behaviour (such as shutting down, interrupting, or counter-accusing) which further block curiosity and learning. Instead, the Insight mediator begins by asking each party to talk about how they hope their lives will improve after talking to each other in the mediation.

'Asking the hope question' is more than simply asking about a hope. It involves a series of communication techniques that reveal and clarify the parties' hopes, motivations and visions for how changing their situation today will improve their lives tomorrow. Using our case study, 'What to do with Mom,' the following dialogue exemplifies the strategy referred to as 'asking the hope question.'

'As I discussed with you in the convening session, I am going to begin the mediation by asking each of you to talk about how you hope opening up the dialogue between you about your Mom will make your lives better tomorrow and in the future. This is a question about your motivation for coming to mediation today rather than what you want to see in terms of an outcome. I will give you a moment to think about this, then ask who would like to go first?'

Carla offers to speak first:
'Okay, Carla, what are you hoping will be better for you tomorrow if you are able to talk to Adrianna today about the things that are concerning you? Once we are sure we understand your hopes Carla, I will ask you, Adrianna, to share your hopes for how

today's mediation can lead to a better tomorrow for you.'

Although mediators who do not identify as Insight practitioners may ask questions about hopes or reasons for coming to mediation, they likely have different intentions. For example, a mediator whose goal is to help the parties discover and negotiate interests may use a question about hopes to reveal negotiable entry points. The goal and strategies of an Insight mediator are quite different. Because an Insight mediator wants to help parties unblock or release their curiosity so that they can learn and discover new possibilities for themselves, a mediator uses the hope question to shift a party's attention away from their own certainty of threat and a repetition of their defend story.

Parties coming to a mediation session have come with their certainties and habitual behaviours. Some may be prepared to fight for what they feel they need or deserve, while others feel stuck. Most parties feel they must convince the mediator that they are right, or that they are the 'wronged' party. In these truncated states, the parties are unlikely to be able to verbalize their hopes even after they are prompted by the mediator to think about this before they arrive to mediation. It is very common when a mediator asks about hopes for a better tomorrow that parties answer with disguised demands or vague generalities: *'I want an apology;' 'I hope she'll stop micro-managing me.'* Other parties may be quite vague: *'I'd like things to be better between us;' 'I'd like some respect.'*

Insight mediators spend time discovering the root of the parties' answers to the hope question as a way to make known that which is often unknown to the parties themselves. Reflecting more deeply on their own, as well as the other's, hopes for the mediation can itself generate a more hopeful environment. Sparked by the mediator's authentic curiosity, this process of discovery and reflection on what really matters offers the parties another opportunity to become less truncated by threat and more open to learn. Hearing another party's hope for a more desirable future in lieu of the unwelcome present can inspire a sense that engaging in the difficult conversations ahead could be worthwhile. Furthermore, because the mediator ensures that each party hears and understands the other's person response to the hope question, it provides an opportunity for the party to shift their own attention away from preparing for rebuttal.

Being transparent about their intentions [7], Insight mediators help the parties articulate a specific, concrete or imaginable response to the question about hopes for a better tomorrow. This helps the party more clearly express their valuing or meaning-making about what matters to them; something that their threat-defend pattern of interaction very often prevents them from realizing. To help the party articulate a concrete response, the Insight mediator uses the communication skill of asking 'layered questions,' whereby they ask a series of questions that each follow from the answer to the previous question.

Let's continue with our case study dialogue to demonstrate this skill. We enter the dialogue after the mediator asks Carla about her hopes for a better tomorrow to which she blurts out: *'I just want Adrianna to do what is best and right for our Mom and stop being so selfish!'*

The mediator then asks a question that follows from this answer:

'You want what's best for your mom. And if Adrianna were to do what you think is best for your Mom, how would this make tomorrow better for you?'

With exasperation Carla answers: 'Well for one thing, Mom would not be alone and then I wouldn't have to worry all the time about her falling and hurting herself!'

The mediator asks a layered question that follows from Carla's answer to the question before: *'You are very worried about your mother's safety and you don't want to worry all the time. So, you're hoping that this conversation will make things better for you in what way?'*

Carla responds: *'Well, I wouldn't have to call and check up on her three times a day or wonder why she hasn't called me back. I'd be able to focus on my own life and deal with my own problems for a change.'*

The mediator uses this information to note that a learning conversation may be possible between the two sisters when their sense of threat is sufficiently diminished: *'So one of the conversations you are hoping to have with Adrianna today involves how to ensure Mom is safe from harm. And that would give you greater peace of mind so you can focus more on your own life. I've made a*

little note for us to come back to that at some point. Before we do that, however, it is important that we hear from Adrianna about what her hopes are for a better tomorrow if we can talk about what matters to her today.'

Before continuing the simulated dialogue between the mediator and Adrianna about her hopes, it is worth noting a few aspects of layered questions. Asking layered questions involves more than asking a sequence of questions (which can sometimes feel to a party like an interrogation rather than an authentically curious conversation). Layered questions usually include a short paraphrase and a targeted question. The short paraphrase helps the mediator verify their under-standing of the party's response, and the targeted question aims to expand or elaborate on the party's thinking about what they said. Layered questions help the parties 'peel back the onion' of their own knowing, valuing and deciding. These kinds of questions ensure the mediator is following the parties' listening and learning, and not their own. For it is not the mediator who needs to know the answer to the questions; it is the party, whose truncated curiosity has prevented the discovery of their own better options.

A second aspect of layered questions is that the strategy of paraphrase and targeted question enables a mediator to explore respectfully a party's concern while recognizing that a party may feel too threatened or truncated to verbalize their hopes. The mediator's goal is to notice and support more curiosity rather than question the parties in a way that could further shut them down. Such is the case with Adrianna in the dialogue below.

The mediator turns toward Adrianna and asks: '*What are you hoping will be better for you Adrianna, if you are able to talk to Carla today about the things that are concerning you? This question is about what motivated you to choose mediation rather than a solution you think would work. Feel free to take a moment to think about this before you answer.*'

Adrianna in a frustrated way says: '*Well I hope that Carla will come to her senses and see there is really only one workable option here. She needs to move in with Mom. It just makes good sense given that Mom is adamant she is fine on her own, but we both know she has taken some spills and needs help. I just don't see the problem! There is plenty of space for Carla in the house, and if she moved in with Mom she would not have to pay rent, which would mean she would no longer worry about having enough money.*'

The mediator asks a layered question: '*For you the solution to the problem seems obvious, which is that Carla move in with your Mom. If this were to happen, how do you envisage your life being better?*'

Adrianna responds: '*It would be better because I would not have to deal with all this ridiculous bickering and stress.*' (Still being accusatory and defensive.)

The mediator asks about hopes once more: '*And if that stress were no longer a part of your life, how might that improve things?*'

Adrianna, still somewhat closed and defensively, says: '*I am not sure what more I can tell you. Clearly if Carla is living with Mom I would worry less about her. And who knows, maybe I would get to see my sister laugh instead of bicker!*'

The mediator recognizes that Adrianna feels frustrated with continuing to be asked about hopes, so does not ask an additional question: '*In addition to being worried about your Mom, it sounds like you would like to have some fun time with your sister.*'.

Having heard from each party what they hope will be better, the mediator has a clearer sense of how to engage the parties in a learning conversation. '*Clearly, Mom's safety is of concern to you both, and you have different ideas about how to support her, and who should do what. You each have a sense of how the future could be better, and my job is help you work through what gets in the way of having a productive conversation so you can move closer to that better future.*'

IN CLOSING

Asking about hopes for an imagined better future early in mediation is an important strategy in Insight Mediation because it expands the parties' ability to think about the preferred future they would like to work toward rather than the unwelcome future they are trying to prevent. In this way, an Insight mediator intentionally uses the opening stages of a mediation to set the foundation for a learning conversation that will generate new insights and ultimately change behaviours.

Instead of inviting parties to make opening statements that are likely to provoke defensive interactions (based on the parties truncated certainty about the other as threat), an Insight mediator uses layered questions to elicit concrete and specific descriptions of a better future. The parties' responses help the mediator assess their openness to engage with each other as well as their motivations for undertaking mediation. With this assessment, the mediator can help the parties have a different kind of conversation that encourages further curiosity towards themselves and the other. Once their flow of curiosity is released, the parties become much more capable of having a conversation to discover what was previously unimaginable.

In future working papers, the remaining three Insight Mediation activities (Deepen Insights, Explore Possibilities and Make Decisions) will be examined in order to point out some of the more distinct and key insight skills and strategies and their relationship to Insight theory.

BOOKS FOR FURTHER READING

Melchin, Kenneth and Cheryl Picard, *Transforming Conflict through Insight*, University Toronto Press, Toronto, 2008.

Picard, Cheryl A., Practising Insight Mediation, University of Toronto Press, Toronto, 2016

NOTES

[1] For simplicity, many Insight mediators call these threats-to-cares.

[2] Picard, *Practising Insight Mediation*, 2016: pp 52-56.

[3] Ibid. p 58.

[4] Ibid. 2016: 60-72.

[5] For a comprehensive discussion of the process-related areas see *Practising Insight Mediation* pp. 60-72.

[6] *Practising Insight Mediation*, pp. 27-33.

[7] Ibid., pp.134-135.

Exploring Expected Futures
Cheryl Picard and Kenneth Melchin, 2023

Insight Mediation offers mediators novel tools and strategies for helping parties transform conflicts by gaining and verifying insights about themselves and others. In this 'working' paper, we illustrate an important Insight Mediation strategy highlighting how it might differ from what other mediators may have learned in their mediation training. To this end, we include an example of a short interaction between the Insight mediator and two sisters, Carla and Adrianna, who are in disagreement about how to support their aging mother. We pick up the conversation at a point during the process of 'deepening the learning conversation' where the mediator is using an Insight strategy known as 'Exploring Expected Futures.'

Exploring Expected Futures is used in situations where the mediator notices parties are remaining locked in their defense-attack behaviours leading to an awareness of the need to shift the pattern of the parties' conversation. The Insight mediator knows that the parties are blocked by feelings of threat and an inability to listen and understand what each other is trying to say. In particular, they are being blocked in their ability to 'learn' anything new about each other. To mitigate this, the mediator responds with the intention of generating new insights as a strategy to deepen the learning that is a prerequisite for conflicting parties deciding to change their conflict behaviour.

In our example of the use of this strategy the mediator's efforts are directed at facilitating a conversation with one sister about what is important to her in such a way that the other sister becomes able to listen without feeling threatened. He does this by probing the threat, not with the intent of remaining focused on the threat, but to help elicit what the sister is protecting as a result of the threat. With this in mind the mediator's questioning and listening is structured to move the conversation so that Carla can listen to Adrianna without feeling the need to defend herself. In other words, the mediator helps Adrianna move through the threat and out the other side. When this happens, Adrianna is able to talk about her own hopes and cares in relation to her own expected futures.

When Adrianna talks about her hopes and cares in relation to her own expected futures, Carla, the listener, is less likely to feel attacked or criticized given that the conversation is no longer focused on attacking her. It has shifted to focus on Adrianna's expected futures in light of her own experiences. As a result of noticing this, Carla's current understanding of the conflict is less likely to be blocked by threat feelings enabling her to begin listening with curiosity. As the mediator is moving through this conversation with Adrianna, he is also paying careful attention to Carla, looking for body language that indicates a shift from a defensive posture to a curious one. After moving through the numerous interventions that form the strategy of Exploring Expected Futures with Adrianna, and verifying that Carla has indeed understood what Adrianna has been saying, the Insight mediator will shift attention to Carla to establish a similar conversation to help her talk about her hopes and cares in relation to her own expected futures, this time with Adrianna listening and coming to feel less attacked or criticized. Once parties are able to have a few experiences of listening and learning without being blocked by threat feelings, they often become able to take over the conversation themselves to pursue novel paths forward. Let's examine the interactions between the Insight mediator and the disputing parties.

NOTICING THE MEDIATOR'S FOCUS

As mentioned previously, our case example involves a conflict between two sisters, Carla and Adrianna, who strongly disagree about how to deal with their aging mother. The mediation has already been going on for a while and attempts by the mediator to shift the attack-defend dialogue between the sisters have not been successful. They continue to speak and respond to each other with attitudes and behaviours that dismiss each other's views. Some of what the mediator is noticing are repetitive explanations of what each party wants, raised voices when they talk to each other, snarky remarks, and other verbal and non-verbal dismissive behaviours.

If you are a mediator trained in another approach, we suggest you pause at this point and consider the situation from the perspective of your prior training. Before proceeding, ask what you would be thinking if you were the mediator. You have already been working with the parties for a while, so you may be feeling some frustration. Perhaps you would want to remind the parties that they agreed to listen and not interrupt each other. Beyond this, you know you need a strategy for moving forward. What strategy would you select? If you were to select a strategy based on your prior training, can you name it and what would it entail? Once you have formulated an answer to this question, read on to see how it would differ or overlap with an Insight mediator's strategy.

In this paper we focused our attention on only one specific Insight Mediation strategy to enable us to better describe and teach the strategy. After noticing the parties continuing to engage in ongoing patterns of defend narratives, the mediator learned that the parties needed help to deepen the learning conversation and decided to respond by using the strategy of Exploring Expected Futures. This strategic choice was due to having observed that both Carla and Adrianna continued to feel threatened through their interactions, and as a result they exhibited little curiosity about what the other was saying verifying that their ability to learn from each other was blocked and that the line of questioning needed to change. Instead of exploring what is important to each party about helping their Mom, the mediator shifted his questioning to focus on their expectations about the future; more specifically what the sisters are trying to prevent from happening in the future. What worries the sisters is exemplified in the mediator's dialogue below and the discussion that follows.

ENTERING THE DIALOGUE

After noticing the parties are stuck in ongoing defend narratives the mediator enters the conversation and says: *'Clearly it is hard right now for either of you to listen to what the other thinks would be best. This is not uncommon in situations where family members are concerned about another family member's welfare. In fact, this difficulty is why you asked for help through mediation. Let me shift the focus of the conversation a bit to see if we can discover what is so threatening and what is making it hard for you to listen to each other. If you are going to be successful making decisions about how to deal with your aging mother it will be helpful to learn what each of you is worried about. Who would like to start?'*

As the older sister, Adrianna offers to begin. The mediator turns to her and says: *'Adrianna, talk a bit about what you would expect a supportive and helpful person or friend would do if you were to share with them your worries about your aging mother.'*

Discussion: The Insight mediator begins the strategy of Exploring Expected Futures by asking Adrianna a question that invites her to shift attention away from the current narrative

about the conflict events and problems. She deliberately asks a question that focuses her attention and the attention of Carla, the listener, in an area that takes the conversation away from events that implicate or blame Carla. Instead, she asks Adrianna about how she imagined the conversation would unfold from her experience of talking to others about things concerning her.

What the mediator does not do is stay in the problem-saturated narrative, as this will sustain parties defend patterns of interacting. Nor does the mediator simply ask what parties care about right now. Instead, he directs attention to future expectations because this is where the deeper, most pressing cares and threats generating the conflict are to be discovered.

Let's continue with the conversation and our analysis. If Adrianna provides new and potentially less accusatory information in response to this question, then the mediator follows up with a question to Adrianna that adds a further layer onto this information. The mediator here is using the micro skill of 'asking layered questions.' [1] Layered questions involve the mediator asking the party an open curious question about the answer that was given to the question that was asked before. Notice in the mediator's paraphrasing below that he avoids attaching blame to Carla for not being supportive of her sister but instead follows up with a question about her interpretation of perceived lack of support: *'You expected the person to trust your thinking on how to deal with your mother at this point in her life, and to be open and supportive of your ideas. What do you hear a person telling you when you are not given the support you expect?'*

Discussion: This layered question begins to deepen the learning conversation by asking Adrianna about the threat she feels when she does not receive the support she expects. Even if the question focuses attention towards a negative expectation, the focus remains on something within Adrianna and not on something that explicitly implicates Carla. This gives Carla 'space' for paying attention to what Adrianna is saying without feeling personally criticized or attacked.

If Adrianna provides information about a possible threat that could be fuelling the conflict, the mediator follows up with another layered question to Adrianna that builds on the first two and deepens by exploring her expected dire future. Notice that the mediator 'paraphrases' [2] what she heard before proceeding to ask another layered question. This skill of paraphrasing first and asking second is what Insight mediators refer to as 'bridging.' [3] *'Clearly there is something quite worrisome for you when you encounter this apparent lack of trust (this is the mediator's interpretation of the party's response to the prior question). What are you imagining will happen if this continues?'*

Discussion: This is an extremely important question because it provides Adrianna with a way of speaking about her feelings of threat in a way that relates, not to Carla, but to her own future expectations. Insight mediators know that usually these future expectations have roots in the party's own past, and she is inviting Adrianna to speak about events in her own past that lead her to expect this dire future outcome. Once again, this places Carla in the position of observing and listening to Adrianna speak about her own threat-to-care narrative. The mediator purposefully does not yet bring Carla into the conversation because she wants to make sure Carla does not feel she has to defend against Adrianna's interpretation of events. Before inviting Carla to speak she wants to allow Adrianna to finish talking about her own fears.

If Adrianna provides information that is expansive rather than contractive, then the mediator once again asks a layered question to deepen further. Asking layered questions to deepen understanding are not simply additive, they intend to provide insight into the essence or core of the threat interpretations leading to defend responses. Recognizing the conversation with Adrianna is at an important junction, the mediator invites Adrianna to speak directly about Carla: *'There is something important about Carla trusting you, Adrianna, that you care deeply about and that you are trying hard to protect. Perhaps you could speak directly to Carla and tell her what is it about your relationship that matters to you so much and what you are afraid of losing.'*

Discussion: With this question, the mediator is giving Adrianna the chance to formulate the positive value that is at the centre of her feelings of threat—the care she feels she is protecting. Through deepening we have learned that this is all about protecting her future relationship with her sister. With this question, the conversation remains detached from blaming Carla in two ways. First, Adrianna's response is an exploration of her own life narrative, a narrative that does not accuse, blame or attack Carla; and second, the question asks about a positive value held by Adrianna rather that a negative disvalue that could be taken as a criticism of Carla.

All through this questioning with Adrianna, the mediator has not only been noticing and listening carefully to her, she has also been carefully observing Carla's reactions. She is interested in knowing whether Carla's body language reveals that she is responding to what Adrianna is saying with attention and curiosity. If so, she may be shifting away from her ongoing stance of attack-defend and is learning something new. If Carla's body language reveals openness and curiosity, the mediator will shift attention to the other party, in this case Carla, and begin Exploring Expected Futures. But, before this happens, it will be important for Carla to verify that she has heard correctly what Adrianna has been saying. The mediator turns to Carla and says something like this: *'Carla, you have been listening attentively to Adrianna talk about what matters to her. It is important for you to share your understanding of what matters to your sister so she can tell you if you have this right or correct what you do not understand. What is your understanding of what matters most to Adrianna?'*

'Now that we know you understand Adrianna, perhaps you would talk about your ideas on how best to deal with your Mom, being sure to let Adrianna know what matters to you and what you are afraid will *happen given that the two of you have not been able to agree on your mother's care. So, let me ask you: What would you expect a supportive and helpful person or friend to do to help you find the best way to deal with your Mom's situation, and if that didn't happen what would you think?'*

Discussion: The mediator continues along this path of deepening the learning until both parties show some genuine interest in what the other is saying. Once both parties become curious about each other they will begin asking questions to expand and deepen what they know and they will stop contradicting each other or dismissing each other's ideas. At this point, the mediator becomes more confident that the parties have, at least for the present, shifted out of their attitudes of attack-defence. They have opened their minds to allow for curiosity and learning from each other. The mediator can now feel relatively confident about engaging in new lines of inquiry that explore possibilities and decision-making for dealing with the parties' aging mother.

To help readers reflect on their understanding of the strategy of Exploring Expected Futures we summarize below the progression of the mediator's interventions moving the parties from their defending behaviours to curious wondering. Two points need highlighting: First, the progression is based on the mediator responding not prescribing, which in Insight Mediation is referred to as 'responsive intentionality.' [4] This behavioural outcome reminds the Insight mediator to be responsive to the parties using theory-informed intention to both the situation and the individual. Our second point underscores that it is questions that lead to insight and learning. And, while the structure of the question matters, the more important aspect is what the question asks about. Whereas some mediation methods focus attention on the discovery of interests or needs, the Insight approach seeks to reveal the threats behind conflict behaviour. Insight mediators engage parties in conversation about whether their feelings of threat are deliberate attacks on what matters to them.

RECAPPING THE USE OF LAYERED QUESTIONS DURING THE STRATEGY OF EXPLORING EXPECTED FUTURES

The series of layered questions in the example below show the progression of the layered questions asked by the mediator during his deepening conversation with Adrianna. We want to point out that the questions are not formulaic; they are a 'dynamic pattern of responses that follow the parties' own storytelling.'

The Insight mediator began by asking Adrianna a curious question that went something like this: *'What do you expect that a supportive or helpful person would do in this particular situation?'*

When Adrianna provided some new inform-ation in response to this question, the mediator followed up with a curious question to Adrianna that added a deeper layer onto this information: *'What do you think a person is telling you when she does not give you this help or support?'*

When Adrianna talked about information that the mediator understood as a threat fuelling the conflict, he followed up with another layered threat-based question, again to Adrianna, that deepened on the first two questions by exploring future expect-ations of threat: *'What is the worry or dire future that you expect to happen when you do not get this help or support?'*

Once again, when Adrianna provided information that moved the conversation forward, the mediator followed up with another layered question to deepen further on future expectations: *'What is it that you are trying to protect when this sort of conversational roadblock happens?'*

When Adrianna is able to provide new information in response to this deeper question that appears to be at the root of her fears, the mediator first verifies that Carla had heard what Adrianna said. He asks: *'Carla, what is your understanding of what Adrianna is envisioning will happen and how she is protecting that it does not happen?'*

All the while through this questioning, the mediator has been directing his questions to Adrianna and he has been listening carefully to Adrianna. As importantly, he has also been observing the reaction of Carla, and whether Carla's words and body language reveal whether she is responding to Adrianna with an attitude of defend-attack or whether she is becoming genuinely curious about what Adrianna is saying. Once it is determined that Carla understands what Adrianna has been saying, and that she is ready to talk about what matters to her and how it is being threatened in the current context, the mediator shifts his attention to deepening on the threat-to-care that Carla feels being sure to also attend to Adrianna's reactions.

CONCLUSION

In this brief text, we have provided an illustration of the Insight Mediation strategy Exploring Expected Futures. Our goal has been to help mediators trained in other approaches identify particular ways that practicing Insight Mediation differs from practices rooted in their prior training. We selected this particular strategy because it highlights how Insight mediators think differently about conflict. Insight Mediation does not understand conflict as arising from incompatible or conflicting positions or interests. Rather it arises when parties' ability to learn from each other in conversations is blocked by feelings of threats-to-cares. To help parties move past these blockages, Insight mediators know

they need to find ways to 'deepen' their learning conversation. This case study illustrates how the Insight Mediation strategy of Exploring Expected Futures helps parties achieve this goal.

BOOKS FOR FURTHER READING

Melchin, Kenneth and Cheryl Picard, *Transforming Conflict through Insight*, University of Toronto Press, Toronto, 2008.

Picard, Cheryl A. *Practising Insight Mediation*, University of Toronto Press, Toronto, 2016.

NOTES

[1] See Picard, *Practising Insight Mediation*, p. 134.
[2] Ibid. pp. 112-123.
[3] Ibid. pp. 139-140.
[4] Responsive intentionality is described in Dr. Picard's book, *Practicing Insight Mediation*, pp. 31-33.

Appendix G

What is the Insight Mediator Looking for?
Ken Melchin, Cheryl Picard, and Mike Stebbins, 2023

INTRODUCTION

A lot of important work has been done, and still remains to be done, to better understand what Insight mediators do to accomplish their goals. Gaining this understanding will be important for the work of training new Insight mediators. In order to prepare this fourth Insight Mediation working paper, Cheryl and Ken invited Mike Stebbins into the conversations. [1] We are grateful for the contributions he brings and look forward to Mike's continued participation.

The focus of this paper is the question of our title: '*What is the Insight mediator Looking for?*' After preparing and discussing a number of draft texts, we formulated the following five points. These points are not meant to be exhaustive. Rather, they represent insights we gained by drawing on Lonergan's self-reflective method to better understand Insight Mediation.

Ken prepared the initial drafts and then the three of us discussed the drafts, making changes along the way. At various moments throughout the paper, we have retained the first-person singular accounts from Ken's original draft in this text. We have named our advanced-level Insight mediator, 'Marie.'

(1) Clarifying the Question: *What Change is the Insight Mediator Looking for that has the Potential to Increase the Probability of Productive End Result?*

We have formulated this question with the assumption that there is indeed some specific 'thing' that our IM mediator, Marie, is looking for, even when she is open to a wide range of different possibilities, and even as she remains careful not to focus on any one particular event. This may sound like a contradiction. But it isn't. So, to clarify, Ken will give you an example illustrating what we mean.

This past weekend I was looking for a way to hang up my backyard bird feeder. The tree I had used last year was damaged in a storm and taken down this past summer. So, I needed an alternative. I began by looking for another tree and I found it. But it didn't have a limb of the right strength at the right height to hang the feeder. So, I made the decision that I will attach something to the tree to hang the feeder. I knew where the feeder needed to be located with respect to the tree trunk. So, I knew I needed something to emulate a branch that would locate the feeder in that spot.

I could have gone online to look for a bird feeder 'hanger' that I could buy. But I decided to see if I could find something in the jumble of stuff I keep around the house. Whenever I do a home repair job (which is often), I always keep all the leftovers. So, I always have a considerable jumble of stuff around in the house and in the garage. I decided to search through this jumble.

I knew what type of result I needed to achieve. But I did not know how I was going to achieve this result. And so, I did not know what sort of object I was looking for in searching through the jumble. Consequently, I had to keep my mind open to a very wide range of data and possible options. If I were to focus my mind on one thing, I knew I would not succeed. I had to pull my mind away from focusing on any one object.

What I did keep clearly focused in my mind, however, was the type of result I needed to achieve. This meant that as I pawed my way through the jumble of stuff, I was examining each object with a very particular question: 'Will this achieve my result?' I examined a wide range of objects and discarded most of them in my pursuit of an answer to my question. Eventually, I hit on an insight: a flag pole holder. I needed one of those flag pole holder brackets that mounts on the side of a house with a short pole that goes up at a 45-degree angle. I found all but one of the pieces in my basement-garage jumble. And I found the final missing piece at my neighbourhood hardware store for a reasonable price. I spent Sunday afternoon mounting my bird feeder.

Thinking back on the operations my mind performed during this process, and thinking ahead to our conversation on Insight Mediation, I discovered that my bird feeder searching was similar to Marie's searching in an Insight Mediation.

We will draw on Bernard Lonergan's philosophy to explain this. We will use Lonergan' terminology with the assumption that, eventually, this may not be the ideal terminology to use when explaining or teaching IM (Insight Mediation).

Lonergan coined the expression, *open heuristic concept* to explain what the mind is doing in asking questions and when searching for understanding. We have 'something specific' in mind when we are searching, but we don't know what it is, so we keep ourselves open to a wide range of data and a wide range of options. Yet the 'something specific' provides the criteria that will tell us when we have found what we're looking for.

This is what we mean when we ask the question: What is Marie looking for when she is mediating? There is an 'open heuristic concept' that is focusing her mind and guiding her searching. In the remaining points, we present some features of this open heuristic concept.

(2) Evoking a Change in the Listener

Part-way through a mediation, our Insight mediator, Marie, is looking to have a conversation with one of the parties—the speaker—that will evoke a change in the other party—the listener. This is important because mediators frequently ask questions in order to gain insights for themselves. At other times, they ask questions in order to evoke insights in the speaker. Marie, however, does not focus on either of these. Rather, she focuses on the listener while he listens to the speaker, and she is focused on the listener gaining an insight that results in a change in his pattern of listening to the speaker.

(3) Threat Feelings as Data

In the third point, we speak about the importance of threat feelings as the data that IM mediators explore. In conflict, parties display threat feelings in their reactions to each other, and it is essential for IM mediators to focus their questioning on these data. We will speak about these data in relation to our question: What is the Insight Mediator Looking for? To clarify, Ken provides a personal observation:

What never ceases to amaze me is that, while my own response to the display of threat feelings in conflict is generally to step away from the threat, Marie's response is always to step towards the threat. I noticed this again during a three-way conversation, in Marie's response to both me and the other participants. The participant's question and my own reply both focused on 'how to get around' the problem posed by a party's display of threat feelings. Marie's reply, on the other hand, was straightforward. The Insight Mediator does not 'get around' the threat feelings. Rather, she moves towards the threat feelings to explore them in order to discover something important.

This 'something important,' we believe, is central to what we are looking for with our question: What is the Insight Mediator Looking for? Marie's searching in a mediation seems to be guided by the assumption that exploring threat feelings achieves the result that is sought. On their own, however, simply naming or describing the threat feelings do not provide insights. IM mediators move into the threats in their questioning, but they move through them and out the other side. We will say more about this further movement in the next two points. But the threat feelings do provide the required data. Insight mediators need to attend to these data, and their questioning needs to focus on the threats.

(4) The Listener's Judgement Changes the Listener

In this fourth point, we speak about the insights that IM mediators seek to evoke in the listening party, notably the *reflective insights or judgements*.

In the past, we spoke about a successful IM mediation as one in which the mediator facilitates a transformation through insight. We've said that her job is to help parties make discoveries that transform their patterns of interaction. Their interaction shifts from a pattern governed by defend-attack responses to one governed by curiosity-cooperation responses.

In the years since the publication of *Transforming Conflict through Insight*, our understanding has developed so that we place more emphasis on the role of 'reflective insights' in this transformative process. In the book we made a distinction between 'direct insights' and 'reflective insights.' [3] Since then, even though we realize that parties do gain direct insights that are important, we now focus more on 'reflective insights' as playing the central role in the transformation.

After the publication of *Insight*, Lonergan shifted his language and used the term 'judgement' in place of 'reflective insight.' When speaking to a wider public, we find that the word 'judgement' usually evokes a range of images and meanings that get in the way of communication. Often the word 'verification' provides a better alternative. But for the present purposes, for purposes of clarity among us, we would like to use the term 'judgement' to refer to this cognitional operation.

We believe that what Marie looks for in a mediation (her open heuristic concept) is a change in the listener that begins to emerge when he makes the judgement that he is no longer certain about his prior understanding of the speaker. This judgement opens him to considering the possibility that his understanding of the other could be wrong in some important way. This 'discovery' is not a direct insight, although it follows on a direct insight. It is not simply new information, although it follows from the disclosure of information that may be new in some way. Rather, it is a judgement. When he understands the 'something new,' he follows this by making the judgement that something important about his prior understanding of the other may not be correct. With this judgement, he becomes open to new information and new insights, and this changes his form of engagement with the other in the conflict.

(5) The Listener's Judgement about the Speaker's Value as Necessary Threat

In this final point, we ask: what special type of judgement has this effect of transforming the listener's pattern of involvement in conflict? There are many different judgements that parties make in a mediation that do not have this effect of transforming the conflict. What makes this special type of judgement different from the others?

We already know that this judgement is to be arrived at by exploring the parties' threat feelings. But we also know that mediators can explore threat feelings in ways that do not lead them to this special type of judgement. What should mediators be looking for to guide them in exploring the threat feelings?

Observing Insight mediators, and thinking back about conversations we've had, we are struck by the way they speak about getting parties focused on the same information about their involvement in the conflict. We have asked ourselves: Same information about what? On each occasion, Marie's questioning evokes one party's articulation of something beneath her threat feelings, and then she turns to the other and asks for his understanding of what she's expressed. She is always looking to get parties to sit up and take notice of the same information. But it seems to be information about what lies behind or beneath the threat feelings. In the strategy, 'Exploring Expected Futures' discussed in Working Paper #3, for example, the mediator sets up this conversation by exploring one party's expected dire future while the second party listens. Then, by asking the listener what he has understood from the first party's account, she is inviting the listener to compare what he just understood with his prior understanding. This can lead to the judgement discussed in the previous point. But our question is: Judgement about what?

We believe the judgement is effective in transforming conflict when it is about the value or disvalue that lies at the heart of the threat feeling. In Lonergan's terms, she is probing the *feeling as intentional response to value. [2]* Her probing seeks to unearth the value at the heart of the feeling. We believe that, in our analysis of the strategy, 'Exploring Expected Futures,' we arrive at a formulation of this objective when we speak about the IM mediator asking the speaker about the value she is protecting. When the listener understands the speaker's articulation of what she is protecting, he is often surprised. 'I never expected that!' This surprise arises because he compares this with his own assessment of her intentions and judges that his prior understanding was not correct.

Here, we believe, is what the IM mediator is looking for. The mediator has created a situation in which the listener can safely listen to the speaker. The listener listens to the speaker answer the mediator's questions as Marie probes expected futures. Eventually, the listener understands something new, something he had not previously understood. *The listener makes the judgement that he is no longer certain that the value the speaker is pursuing or protecting necessarily threatens what is important to him.*

What is important for transforming the conflict is that the listener's judgement has a direct impact on his own threat feelings. Once the speaker is judged to be pursuing or protecting a sufficiently different value, one that does not actually threaten the value the listener has been protecting, the listener's own threat feelings begin to dissipate. The speaker's actions are not focused on harming him, they have a different objective. With this judgement, the listener experiences a release from his own need to protect something that is important for him. The speaker's actions do not aim at harming his own 'something important,' the value that underlies his own pursuits.

Our threat feelings arise because of what we understand and judge about the value that the other is pursuing or protecting. We have our own values that evoke our feelings, and when these values are threatened, we shift into defend-attack mode. In conflict, it is our interpretation of what the other is pursuing or protecting that threatens our values. When we make the judgement that our interpretation is not necessarily correct, this has an impact on our own threat feelings. Often enough this results in our threat feelings beginning to dissipate.

REFERENCES

Melchin, Kenneth R. and Cheryl A. Picard, *Transforming Conflict through Insight,* Toronto: University of Toronto Press, 2008.

Picard Cheryl A., *Practicing Insight Mediation,* Toronto: University of Toronto Press, 2016.

NOTES

[1] Working papers 1, 2, and 3 can be found on the *Insight Today* blog at: https://www.insighttodayonline.com

[2] See *Transforming Conflict through Insight* pp. 84-90, and *Practising Insight Mediation* pp. 44-47.

[3] We also spoke about 'inverse insights.' Since then, we no longer use the term 'inverse insight' because we do not think it helps clarify what the mediator is doing.

About the Author

Dr Cheryl Picard, Emeritus Professor at Carleton University in Ottawa, is a pioneer of the Insight approach to conflict and mediation. With more than four decades of experience as a conflict practitioner and mediator, she is widely recognized for her ability to bridge theory and practice. A true "pracademic," Dr. Picard is known for facilitating learning that is theoretically grounded and deeply experiential, reflective, and transformative. She is the author of Practicing Insight Mediation (2016) and co-author, with Dr. Ken Melchin, of Transforming Conflict through Insight (2008).

Author's Note

I hope this Insight Mediation Learning Guide advanced your knowledge and answered many of your questions, even perhaps quieted some of your doubts. Since its inception in the early 2000s the practice of Insight Mediation has expanded globally. Research continues and books and journals are now on the shelf. Unfortunately, high quality workshop training materials are scarce. I set out to change this.

This Learning Guide provides trainers and their learners with a practical and accessible resource. It can also be used to supplement materials used to teach conflict and mediation courses in college and university. To this end, key Insight Mediation terms are defined and include examples of how they might sound in real life. Reference to page numbers from my book Practising Insight Mediation will help you find deeper explanations of both theory and practice. Numerous individual or group practice activities help students deepen their skills. Given there is an array of conflict in day-to-day life, I left it with you, the trainer, to select the conflict contexts that best suit your experience and the needs of your learners. Finally, the material is organized so you can design sessions of varying lengths—from short, focused modules to multi-day workshops, and integrate your own creativity and expertise.

Perhaps surprising may be the inclusion of five recent 'working papers' written by prominent Insight researchers. Including these practice-oriented pieces that examine specific aspects of the Insight approach was to make available recent leading-edge thinking to broaden and deepen your understanding of Insight's structure and value. My hope is the papers and this Guide will equip you to teach this promising new method of understanding and engaging with conflict through learning. I wish you success on your Insight journey.

Cheryl A. Picard PhD,
Prince Edward Island, 2026

www.ingramcontent.com/pod-product-compliance
Lightning Source LLC
Chambersburg PA
CBHW060803270326
41926CB00003B/81